On Your Bike
Yorkshire Dales

— ✸ —

Andy Corless

GW00418646

Other areas covered by the *On Your Bike* series
from Countryside Books include:

BRISTOL & BATH

CAMBRIDGESHIRE

CHESHIRE

THE CHILTERNS

THE COTSWOLDS

DERBYSHIRE & NOTTINGHAMSHIRE

DEVON

ESSEX

HERTFORDSHIRE & BEDFORDSHIRE

LANCASHIRE

LEICESTERSHIRE & RUTLAND

LINCOLNSHIRE

NORFOLK & SUFFOLK

SOMERSET

SURREY

SUSSEX

THAMESSIDE

On Your Bike
Yorkshire Dales

Andy Corless

COUNTRYSIDE BOOKS
NEWBURY, BERKSHIRE

COUNTRYSIDE BOOKS
3 Catherine Road
Newbury, Berkshire

To view our complete range of books,
please visit us at
www.countrysidebooks.co.uk

ISBN 978 1 84674 031 2

Designed by Graham Whiteman
Cover photo showing Muker
supplied by Derek Forss

Photographs by the author
Maps by Gelder Design & Mapping

Produced through MRM Associates Ltd., Reading
Typeset by CJWT Solutions, St Helens
Printed by Cambridge University Press

CONTENTS

AREA MAP SHOWING THE LOCATIONS OF THE RIDES

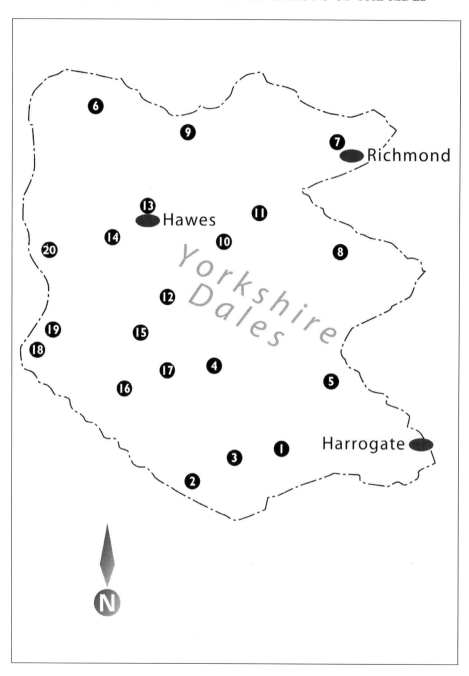

INTRODUCTION

Since becoming a National Park in 1954, the Yorkshire Dales has grown both in popularity and accessibility. Yorkshire is England's biggest county and offers a broad diversity of country lanes suitable for cycling, including its own regional cycling network. The landscape is spectacular, rugged and full of interest. This all makes for wonderful cycling country and the rides in this book include visits to the highest pub in England at Tan Hill, with views across miles of open moorland all around, How Stean Gorge, Aysgarth Falls, Malham Cove and Buttertubs Pass. The routes pass through Wensleydale, Wharfedale, Bishopdale and Coverdale, rising and falling with the landscape and travelling country lanes past waterfalls and limestone crags. Along the way, why not stop off to visit Jervaulx Abbey, Bolton Castle or the Embsay and Bolton Steam Railway, or explore Richmond, Skipton, Pateley Bridge or any other of the picturesque and historic towns and villages through which you will pass?

This is an area where you will still find more sheep than people, and where the village shops do well to survive in these days of supermarkets and internet shopping. There are plenty of places to find refreshments now, as well as popular tourist attractions and, more recently, National Park Centres. The 20 circular rides are based primarily on the National Park, ranging from 12 to 33 miles in length. A fit racing cyclist could complete some of these rides in under an hour, but that isn't the point! You can take all day, if you wish, to complete one ride and there are plenty of inns, B&Bs and hotels in the area as well as the various youth hostels should you decide to group some of the rides together to form the basis of a few days' touring. The location chosen for each of the rides is designed for easy accessibility and to provide long-stay parking facilities should you decide to travel to the area by car.

Some of the rides are hillier than others, particularly in the north of the National Park around Wensleydale and Swaledale, and I recommend that you should be confident of your ability as a cyclist before tackling these routes and having to handle the steep ascents and descents associated with the Yorkshire Dales.

Finally, enjoy yourself and make your time and effort worthwhile!

Andy Corless

GUIDE TO USING THIS BOOK

Each route is preceded by details to help you:

The **route title** and **introduction** give an overview of the area to be covered on the ride, including particular features to look out for, and the total mileage.

The **maps** listed are all Ordnance Survey maps from the 1:50,000 Landranger series. These particular maps, as well as the 1:25,000 Explorer maps, will be well worthwhile purchasing as the sketch maps can give only limited information and are not entirely to scale.

The grid reference for the **starting point** is given, and an indication of long-stay parking facilities. Places for **refreshment** along the route are mentioned, some of them particular pubs or cafés that are cyclist-friendly but there are plenty of such establishments throughout the Yorkshire Dales. The note on the **route** will give you some idea of how difficult you should expect the ride to be, particularly those involving steep ascents and descents. You should be aware, of course, that the Yorkshire Dales is a hilly region, particularly between Wensleydale and Swaledale.

THE ROUTES

One of the advantages of using this guide is that the route details refer to what you will see on the road. I have personally ridden all of the routes, taking notes of signposting, the names of roads, and identifying visible features to help ensure that those following the routes will not get lost. You should bear in mind, however, that things can change over time – cafés or pubs may close, roads may be closed for repair, for instance, though every care has been taken to be accurate.

The rides have been arranged by geographical location rather than by their relative length or the ease or difficulty of the terrain to be encountered. Route descriptions are kept simple. Instructions to go left or right are printed in bold type: **turn L**, **turn R**. A sketch map tracing the suggested ride gives you a general idea of the route to follow, but more detail will be found on the recommended OS maps.

At the end of each ride there are brief details of places of interest. I suggest you read this section before embarking on the ride or you may regret what you have missed!

COMFORT AND SAFETY

For your safety on these rides it is important that your bicycle is in a roadworthy condition and that you and your companions, if any, are competent bike-handlers and familiar with the rules of the road. I suggest you read the Highway Code's 'Extra Rules for Cyclists' before embarking on any of these cycling journeys.

The intricate network of Yorkshire lanes and country roads offers cyclists the opportunity of exploring some of Yorkshire's finest landscapes. The majority of the rides have been devised in order to take maximum advantage of these quiet roads. Inevitably I have had to include some A-roads on the routes but these have been kept to a minimum, so riders should be aware of the potential dangers, including the steep hills associated with the Yorkshire Dales, where sometimes you will be far from towns or villages and perhaps outside the range of mobile phones.

Wear clothing that can be easily seen – bright fluorescent colours are best, with reflective strips attached, that are easily visible to other road users. Avoid tight clothing; it should either be loose, without flapping too much, or of a stretchy fabric. I would advise you to take a complete set of waterproofs in case it rains as the Yorkshire Dales can prove to be unpredictable, even throughout the summer months. A simple first aid kit and sun protection are also important.

I would also advise you to carry a tool kit in case you need to carry out roadside repairs. Items such as a pump, puncture repair kit, tyre levers and spare inner tubes really are the bare minimum.

One can run out of energy very quickly on a bicycle, so I recommend you should take some form of food and drink with you. Two water bottles, one with an isotonic drink and the other filled with water to pour over your head, is a good idea, along with some energy bars. That should be adequate to get you through the patches when there are no cafés or pubs available.

Above all, enjoy a safe, trouble-free ride.

1
Bolton Priory and Wharfedale
23 miles

A route that presents Wharfedale at its best, this circuit of the villages around the north of Skipton is very popular with cyclists. The ride is full of interest whilst using mainly B-roads and country lanes, following the Yorkshire Cycle Way and the River Wharfe for part of the journey. After leaving Skipton Castle, the route heads past the Embsay and Bolton Steam Railway on our way to Bolton Abbey and the Strid, a beautiful narrow gorge on the River Wharfe. There are panoramic views across some of Yorkshire's finest rugged landscapes and terrain. After passing Bolton Priory, with its 12th century ruins, the ride returns to Skipton through picturesque little villages.

Maps: OS Landrangers 103 Blackburn and Burnley, 104 Leeds and Bradford and 98 Wensleydale and Upper Wharfedale (GR 991519).

Starting point: Skipton Castle. There is a car park near the castle.

Refreshments: Skipton has plenty of cafés and pubs where you can obtain food and drink. There are cafés in almost every village along the route including Burnsall and Cracoe, as well as at Bolton Priory.

The route: This is the more difficult of the two rides from Skipton (see Route 2), with some steep climbs, particularly between Bolton Priory and Cracoe. However, the final 7 miles from Cracoe back to Skipton on the B6265 are relatively flat.

At the roundabout outside Skipton Castle, take the **first exit** onto the A6131 (signposted Bolton Abbey) and continue for ½ mile, then **turn L** onto a minor road (signposted Embsay). In Embsay village where the road splits,

fork R onto Shires Lane (signposted Bolton Abbey) and continue for ¼ mile to a T-junction. **Turn R** (signposted Halton East/Bolton Abbey).The route now follows a minor road for the next 4½ miles, the first 2 miles of which are through

The 12th century church of St Wilfred , Burnsall

rolling pastureland. After Halton East you break out into the open, affording panoramic views across to some of Yorkshire's finest rugged scenery, culminating with a welcome descent into Bolton Abbey.

On arriving at the T-junction opposite the tearoom cottage, **turn L** onto the B6160 (signposted Priory) and continue for ½ mile to Sandholme. In between, you can look back and admire the ruins of Bolton Priory off to your right. **Turn R** into Sandholme and descend to the

parking area. *Here, you'll have the opportunity of some welcome refreshments at the café opposite the footbridge before tackling the toughest section of the ride.*

Leave the café via the footbridge (signposted Valley of Desolation) and continue as far as the crossroads opposite Bolton Park Farm. **Turn L** onto a minor road and proceed for 4½ miles, climbing two short, steep hills to a T-junction. As you climb the hills, on your left-hand side are views of Yorkshire at its best as you follow the River Wharfe – but

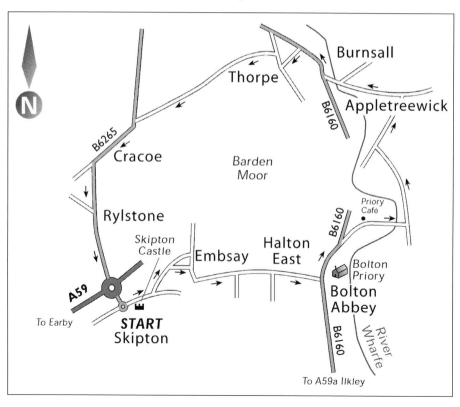

Burnsall village

be careful as the road is mostly unfenced.

Turn L onto another minor road (signposted Appletreewick) and proceed for 2½ miles, passing through Appletreewick village, to the T-junction with the B6160 at Burnsall. The village is one of the prettiest in this part of Yorkshire and has a café to your left opposite the T-junction.

Turn R onto the B6160 and in 1¼ miles, **turn L** onto a minor road (blue cycle route signpost), easily identifiable by the *6' 6" – Except for Access* signpost just after the junction. Now engage your lowest gear to climb a hill before descending into the village of Thorpe. Where the road splits, **turn R** and in 50 yards, **turn R** at the T-junction (opposite the postbox) to climb out of the village. In 250 yards, **turn L** onto a minor road and continue for 2½ miles (be careful on this road as parts are very thin with grass in the middle!) to a T-junction with the B6265.

Turn L onto the B6265. In ¼ mile there's a café on the left (Cracoe Café) if you want more refreshments. Continue on the B6265 for 6 miles until you reach the roundabout with the A59 north of Skipton. This 6-mile stretch can get quite busy as Lancashire's most distinguished feature, Pendle Hill, comes into view on the horizon, so be careful!

At the roundabout take the **second exit** to continue on the B6265 (signposted Skipton) to return to Skipton Castle.

* *

SKIPTON

Skipton is the gateway to the Yorkshire Dales. The town is full of historical interest and the castle, which is open to the public every day, dates back to Norman times. William Fitzduncan attacked it in 1138 but later married Alice de Romille, whose family built the castle. In the 14th century it became the property of the Clifford family. During the Civil War, in 1649, the castle was partially demolished, and later rebuilt by Lady Anne Clifford. Many of the attractive buildings in Skipton date back to the 14th century. The church of the Holy Trinity, originally 12th century, contains many interesting features including tombs and memorials of the Clifford family. Skipton has always been a very popular market town, receiving its first charter in 1204. Market days are Monday, Wednesday, Friday and Saturday and the market stalls are situated on the main street just to the south of the castle. A later claim to fame is that Lord Moran, the physician to

Winston Churchill, was the son of a local doctor and grew up in the town.

BOLTON ABBEY

The little village of Bolton Abbey is in one of the most popular areas of this part of Yorkshire. The main attraction, the Priory, was founded by Alice de Romille in the 1150s but took a century to complete. Most of the structure now lies in ruins, having been dissolved by Henry VIII in 1539, but the nave has served as the parish church for centuries. The picturesque Bolton bridge, where the A59 crosses the River Wharfe, is just downriver, while upstream is the Strid, a lovely narrow gorge.

BURNSALL

Burnsall stands on the River Wharfe and the 12th century church of St Wilfrid testifies to the antiquity of the village. Anglo-Saxon relics, among them the font, date back beyond the 8th century. The most interesting structure in Burnsall is the five-arch bridge that crosses the Wharfe. Sir William Craven built the original bridge in 1612 after returning to his birthplace in Yorkshire from London, where he had been Lord Mayor since 1610.

2

Elslack Moor and Cravendale

24 miles

A scenic circuit around the villages to the west of Skipton, with some hills early on as the route passes over Elslack Moor. Then you stray into Lancashire for a while, the ride offering spectacular views across to Pendle Hill and the distant Yorkshire Dales. After crossing back into Yorkshire on the short main-road climb out of Earby, the route returns to Skipton using mainly country lanes and following the Leeds and Liverpool Canal for part of the journey.

Map: OS Landranger 103 Blackburn and Burnley (GR 991519).

Starting point: Skipton Castle. There is a car park near the castle.

Refreshments: Skipton has a number of cafés and pubs, and en route there are cafés at Earby and Gargrave.

The route: There are a few testing climbs in the opening miles as the ride passes over Elslack Moor. After Thornton-in-Craven, the route returns to the flat lands of Cravendale.

From the castle, leave the roundabout by taking the **second exit** and continue to the next roundabout, where you take the **third exit**, followed by an immediate **turn R** (signposted Burnley). Continue to the mini-roundabout outside Morrison's, where you go straight on. On reaching the railway station you will see a road off to the right (signposted Carleton). **Turn R** here and climb to the top of the hill. Follow the road around to the left and cross over the railway bridge. Continue to the crossroads with Brookland Terrace, where you **turn R**. Proceed for about ½ mile, passing the crematorium.

Where the road splits shortly after passing under a road bridge, **fork R** (signposted Carleton) and continue to Carleton-in-Craven village. Just after the village sign, follow the road around to the right (signposted Carleton/Colne). Continue through the village, following the signposts for Colne, and shortly after passing the turn-off for Beech Hill Road, engage your lowest gear to climb the hill out of the village.

The ride now follows this minor road for the next 4 miles or so. It's a long climb to the top of the hill, over a mile, but once the gradient eases it is a pleasant ride over Elslack Moor. Just after you begin your descent, **turn R** (signposted Earby). You will now be rewarded for all your hard work out of Carleton by a panoramic descent into Earby,

but be very careful as the gradient is steep in parts!

On your arrival in Earby, continue on the same road that becomes School Lane, and on arriving at the T-junction, **turn R**. There's no signpost but this is the A56 so be careful of traffic. Continue for about 1 mile and on into Thornton-in-Craven. On reaching the junction opposite the clock at the top of the hill, **turn L** (signposted Barnoldswick /Thornton Hall Farm Country Park).

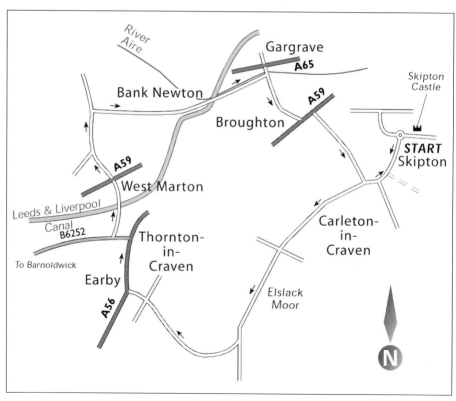

The entrance to Skipton Castle

In about ½ mile, **turn R** (signposted West Marton). The ride now follows a series of minor roads and country lanes virtually all the way back to Skipton. Continue on this road for about 2 miles, passing over the Leeds and Liverpool Canal at one point. When you reach the crossroads with the A59 at West Marton, go straight on. Continue for another 2 miles and where the road divides, just after a short descent to 'R. Metcalfe & Son' at Stainton Hall, follow the road round to the right (signposted Gargrave/Skipton).

Continue on this road now all the way to Gargrave. It is relatively flat (with one or two short hills!) and passes through the village of Bank Newton until reaching the T-junction beside the Masons Arms in Gargrave. *Should you require refreshments, turn L to visit the village, where you will find several places serving food and drink, then retrace your route to the junction.*

For the main route, **turn R** (signposted Broughton). The ride now follows an undulating minor road for the next 2 miles, beginning with an ascent out of Gargrave village before eventually arriving at a T-junction with the A59 at Broughton, where **turn L** (signposted Skipton). Be careful on this stretch of road as it can be busy at times.

After 1 mile, **turn R** (signposted Carleton). Proceed for about 1½ miles to return to Carleton-in-Craven and on arriving at the traffic island beside the Swan Inn, **turn L** (signposted Skipton). Proceed along this road and where the road divides on leaving the village, follow the road round to the left (signposted Skipton) and continue, ignoring all turns, for about 1½ miles. At traffic lights **turn L** (signposted Town Centre) and continue to the roundabout, where you **turn L** to return to the castle.

The Leeds & Liverpool Canal at Bank Newton

EARBY
Earby was once at the centre of a thriving lead mining industry and the Museum of Yorkshire Dales Lead Mining is housed in the old grammar school. The museum opened in 1971 and displays mine tubs, plans and a collection of photographs; it has limited opening times.

THORNTON-IN-CRAVEN
This village stands on the main A56 Colne to Skipton road. The original records of the 12th century church of St Mary were accidentally burnt by a retiring rector, and the first manor house was destroyed by Royalist soldiers during the Civil War after Oliver Cromwell had attended a wedding here! The Pennine Way passes through, offering views of Airedale and distant Pendle Hill.

LEEDS AND LIVERPOOL CANAL
The longest canal in northern England, it was first opened in the 1770s to carry coal, stone, lead etc to the manufacturing cities. By the 1970s it had decayed, but then found a new lease of life as a leisure facility.

3

Embsay and Barden Tower

25 miles

From Gargrave, the opening few miles to Skipton are mainly along minor roads and country lanes, before the ride heads into the Yorkshire Dales, following the Yorkshire Dales Cycle Way for much of the time. The Embsay and Bolton Steam Railway and the 15th century Barden Tower are just two of the attractions along the way. You could add this ride to Route 2 if you were feeling particularly energetic, as the opening few miles duplicate those at the end of that outing.

Maps: OS Landranger 103 Blackburn and Burnley, 104 Leeds and Bradford and 98 Wensleydale and Upper Wharfedale (GR 932542).

Starting point: The Dalesman Café on the corner of the A65 and West Street in Gargrave village. There are two car parks in the village, one of which offers free parking.

Refreshments: The Dalesman Café in Gargrave is popular with cyclists. En route, you will find cafés/tearooms in Skipton, Embsay, Burnsall and Cracoe, all welcoming cyclists, as well as the many village pubs serving food.

The route: The terrain is varied and not too difficult although there are two climbs to be aware of – the ascent out of Gargrave village right at the start and the climb after Eastby.

Leave Gargrave on Church Street (signposted Broughton) and follow this undulating minor road for the first 2 miles. It's a climb to begin with, which starts just after the railway station.

On arriving at the T-junction with the A59, **turn L** (signposted Skipton). Be careful on this stretch of road, as it can be busy at times. After 1 mile, **turn R** (signposted Carleton). Proceed for 1½ miles to Carleton-in-Craven and on arriving at the traffic island beside the Swan Inn,

The Dalesman café at Gargrave

turn L (signposted Skipton/Crematorium). Proceed along this road and where the road splits on leaving the village, follow it around to the left (signposted Skipton) and continue, ignoring all turns, for about 1½ miles.

When you reach a set of traffic lights, **turn L** (signposted Town Centre). The next part of the ride passes through Skipton town centre so take extra care in the increased traffic. Continue until you reach a roundabout, where

turn R (signposted Leeds A65). Very shortly you will come to another roundabout, where **turn L** (**first exit**, signposted Skipton Castle). Continue to the next roundabout outside the castle and **turn R** (**second exit**, signposted Skipton Castle). In about ½ mile **turn L** onto a minor road (signposted Embsay) and continue to Embsay village. As you climb the hill through Embsay you will come to a junction where the road splits. **Fork L** (signposted Eastby/Barden). Continue through the village for about another ¼ mile and **turn L** onto Kirk Lane (signposted Eastby/Barden/Pateley Bridge). This road subsequently becomes Barden Lane in Eastby village.

Proceed straight through Eastby, ignoring all turns, and on leaving the village engage lowest gear to climb the short hill. It's very steep with a couple of hairpin bends but the gradient eases as you break out into the open. Shortly after crossing the cattle grid, you will be rewarded for all your hard work with a long

descent and it's here that you enter the Yorkshire Dales National Park.

Continue until you reach the T-junction with the B6160, where **turn L** (signposted Burnsall/Grassington) and carry on into Barden. This is where you get your first sight of Barden Tower directly ahead. Continue on the B6160 for a further 3 miles to Burnsall. There is a café here as well as a pub serving food if you should want to stop. Continue on the B6160 for a further 1¼ mile and **turn L** onto a minor road

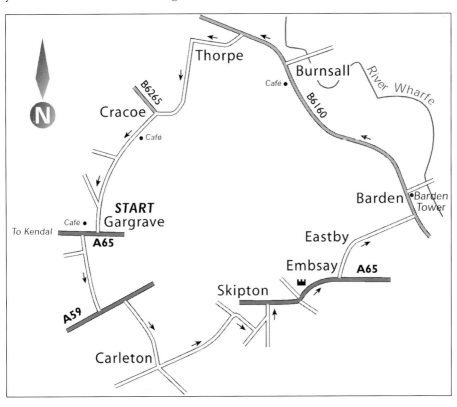

(blue cycle route signpost), easily identifiable by the *6' 6" – Except for Access* signpost just after the junction. Now engage lowest gear to climb a hill before descending into Thorpe village and where the road divides, **turn R**. In 50 yards, **turn R** at the T-junction, opposite the postbox, to climb out of the village. In about 250 yards, **turn L** onto a minor road. The ride now follows this road for the next 2½ miles, but be extremely careful as it is in parts very narrow with grass growing down the middle!

On arriving at the T-junction with the B6265, **turn L** (blue cycle route signpost) and continue into Cracoe village. As you ride through the village you will see a café on your left. Continue along the B6265 and about 250 yards beyond Cracoe Café there is a slip road off to your right (signposted Hetton/Gargrave); **turn R** here.

The route now follows undulating minor roads all the way back to Gargrave. There is a level crossing along this road, so take care. After

The 15th century Barden Tower

about 4 miles you reach a T-junction where **turn L** (signposted Gargrave/Skipton/Settle). Continue for a further ½ mile and shortly after the Gargrave village entrance signpost, **turn R** (signposted Cycle Route 68 – blue sign) and go on to a T-junction where **turn L** to return to the café.

. . . .

EMBSAY AND BOLTON STEAM RAILWAY

The Embsay and Bolton Steam Railway runs on 1¼ miles of track and has three stations: Halton East, Honeywell Halt and Bolton Abbey. Thomas the Tank Engine often runs on the track on a Sunday. It is run by volunteers from the Yorkshire Dales Railway Museum Trust.

BARDEN TOWER

Barden Tower was built by Lord Henry Clifford in 1485 as a hunting lodge and he preferred to live here rather than at Skipton Castle. Lady Anne Clifford had the tower restored in the 1650s after the Civil War.

CRACOE

The 17th century longhouses in the village were built of stone quarried locally on Cracoe and Rylstone Fell. On top of the fell, 1,600 ft above sea level, is a cairn raised in memory of the men from the area who died in the First World War, constructed in the 1920s.

4
Airedale and Kilnsey Crag
33 miles

This ride might be relatively long, with a testing stretch between Malham and Arncliffe, but the scenery is fantastic as you take to the flatter roads of Littondale and Wharfedale on the way to Kilnsey Crag, a limestone scar that juts out spectacularly over the little village nearby. The route takes in both Malhamdale and Wharfedale, with the opportunity to visit lovely Malham Cove and Malham Tarn, as well as the popular market town of Grassington on the Leeds and Liverpool Canal and its nearby picturesque villages before returning to Gargrave.

Maps: OS Landranger 103 Blackburn and Burnley and 98 Wensleydale and Upper Wharfedale (GR 932542).

Starting point: The Dalesman Café on the corner of the A65 and West Street in Gargrave. There are car parks nearby, one of which offers free parking.

Refreshments: The Dalesman Café welcomes cyclists. En route, there are several cafés in Malham, a tearoom and a pub serving food in Arncliffe, and cafés in Kilnsey, Grassington and Cracoe as well as several other country pubs along the way.

The route: The terrain is varied throughout. A hilly section between Malham and Arncliffe is followed by a flatter but undulating ride through Wharfedale.

From the café, **turn L** onto West Street and in 150 yards, **fork L** to remain on West Street. Ride over the bridge and where the road splits, **turn R** onto Cycle Route 68 (signposted Malham/Grassington) and continue to a T-junction opposite Eshton Road Camping and Caravanning Site where you **turn L**.

Continue for about ¾ mile until the road divides, where **fork L** (signposted Malham/Eshton). The route now follows this minor

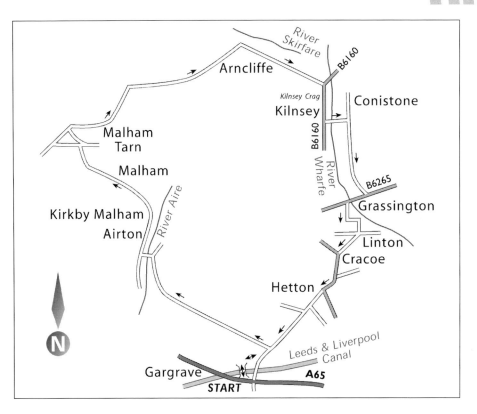

road for the next 6 miles. It becomes the Yorkshire Cycle Way shortly after passing Eshton Hall, which was visible off to your right from the junction. Pass through Airton and Kirkby Malham villages before arriving at Malham, where Malham Cove is instantly recognisable ahead as you descend into the village.

There are a couple of cafés here – one in the National Park Centre – if you require refreshments before tackling the toughest section of the ride.

Ride through the village and where the road splits, **fork L** (signposted Malham Tarn/Arncliffe) and engage lowest gear to climb the hill out of the village. Continue on this road for 2¾ miles until you reach a crossroads. Malham Tarn is visible now off to your right. Continue straight on (signposted Arncliffe) and in ½ mile, **bear R** (signposted Arncliffe). *To visit Malham Tarn Field Centre:* ***turn R*** *onto a signposted drive, which becomes a bridleway after a gate.*

For the main route: continue on this road towards Arncliffe. At about the halfway point you will have to dismount as the road is gated! On reaching Arncliffe, ride through the village and at the T-junction by Mitton Cottage, **turn R** (signposted Kilnsey/Grassington). The route now takes to flatter roads for the next 3 miles through an area known as Littondale.

At the T-junction with the B6160, **turn R** (signposted Grassington/Skipton). Ride on into Kilnsey, where the unmistakable Kilnsey Crag overhang towers above. On leaving the village, **turn L** onto a minor road (signposted Conistone) and ride on into Conistone village, where you **fork R** at the traffic island (signposted Grassington). The route now follows the Kettlewell to Grassington back road for the next 3 miles.

On arriving at the T-junction in Grassington, **turn R** onto the B6265 (signposted Cracoe/Skipton) and in ¼ mile, just after crossing the bridge over the River Wharfe, **turn L** onto a minor road (signposted Linton/Burnsall). Continue for ½ mile, follow the road as it

The limestone scar of Kilnsey Crag seen from across the water

Kilnsey Crag dominates the surrounding countryside

bends around to the right and climb the short steep hill to the crossroads. Continue straight on to join the B6265 (signposted Linton/Cracoe/Skipton) and ride into Linton, known as one of the bonniest villages in Yorkshire! Continue for 1 mile to a T-junction where **turn L** (no signpost) and continue to Cracoe.

Carry on along the main B6265 road and on leaving the village, **fork R** onto a minor road (signposted Hetton/Gargrave). The route now follows undulating minor roads all the way back to the finish. This road has a level crossing to be wary of, as well as some narrow sections so take

care! After about 4 miles you reach a T-junction, where you **turn L** (signposted Gargrave/Skipton/Settle). Continue for a further ½ mile and shortly after the Gargrave village entrance signpost, **turn R** (signposted Cycle Route 68 – blue sign) and continue to a T-junction, where you **turn L** to return to the café.

GARGRAVE
This former market town stands on the Leeds and Liverpool Canal, about 4 miles north-west of Skipton, and where once lead from local mines was loaded onto barges, now pleasure craft moor in

the locks. The church of St Andrew is mostly Victorian but has a 16th century tower – the original church was destroyed by the Scots in 1318. In the south-east corner of the churchyard, beneath a large cross, lies buried Iain Norman Macleod, an MP born in Skipton in 1913 and whose sudden death just after he had been appointed Chancellor of the Exchequer in 1970 shocked the political world.

MALHAM

This pretty limestone village lies amidst spectacular scenery, including the great white cliff of Malham Cove. and Malham Tarn, a natural lake. See Route 17 for more details.

LITTONDALE

This lovely little dale, following the course of the River Skirfare, has long been popular with writers – Charles Kingsley called it Vendale, Wordsworth named it Amerdale, and it was the original setting for the television soap opera Emmerdale Farm!

5

Pateley Bridge and How Stean Gorge

32 miles

This ride explores the eastern Dales in an area known as Nidderdale. One of the more challenging scenic rides in this book, the route passes several reservoirs and also provides the opportunity to visit the spectacular How Stean Gorge before returning to Pateley Bridge, the 'capital' of Nidderdale and an ancient market town in a beautiful setting.

Map: OS Landranger 99 Northallerton and Ripon (GR 157654).

Starting point: Pateley Bridge car park which is to the west of the bridge crossing the River Nidd, opposite the Q8 garage.

Refreshments: There are cafés and pubs in Pateley Bridge. En route there are cafés at How Stean Gorge, Masham and Kirkby Malzeard and also pubs in Ramsgill, Lofthouse and Grewelthorpe, all serving food.

The route: There is a steep climb out of Lofthouse and a long climb from Masham to Grewelthorpe and again from Laverton. Low gears will be an asset on this ride.

Turn L out of the car park (signposted Bishopgate House) and on reaching the junction beside the petrol station, **turn R** onto Low Wath Road (signposted Ramsgill/Lofthouse/Middlesmoor. The ride now follows this minor road for about 6½ miles all the way to Lofthouse, much of it passing Gouthwaite Reservoir and with no serious hills to climb. At Lofthouse village you arrive at a junction beside the Crown Hotel inn.

*To visit How Stean Gorge: continue straight on (signposted Stean/Middlesmoor) and in about ¼ mile **turn L** (signposted How Stean Gorge) and continue to How Stean. After your visit, come back to the junction in Lofthouse beside the Crown Hotel and **turn L** to rejoin the main route.*

The main route: **turn R** at the Crown Hotel (signposted Masham) and engage lowest gear

Leighton Reservoir

to climb out of the village. The climb lasts about 2 miles and is steep to begin with but gradually levels out. You will know when you reach the top, as you pass over a cattle grid as Leighton Reservoir appears on the horizon. It is at this point that you commence your descent towards Masham, passing the reservoir (which is split into two parts) and through the villages of Healey and Fearby, eventually arriving at a T-junction with the A6108 in Masham. **Turn R** (signposted Ripon/Masham) and on reaching the junction beside Wensleydale

Garage, **turn R** (signposted Market Place/Swinton/ Grewelthorpe). At the next T-junction, **turn R** to enter Masham town centre market place.

Follow the road round to the right (signposted Swinton/ Grewelthorpe) and continue on this minor road for the next 3 miles or so, as far as the village of Grewelthorpe. On reaching the Crown Inn, **turn R** and shortly you come to a T-junction, where **turn L** (signposted Kirkby Malzeard/Pateley Bridge).

Continue on this road, ignoring the left turn to Kirkby Malzeard in about 1 mile, to a T-junction. *If you want refreshments, **turn L** into the town.*

For the main route: **turn R** (signposted Dallowgill/Pateley Bridge) and continue to Laverton, where **turn R** opposite the church (signposted Pateley Bridge). In about ½ mile, **turn R** at a T-junction (signposted Pateley Bridge).

The ride now follows minor roads all the way back to Pateley Bridge. Continue on this road for about 3¾ miles. There is a pub on the right, the Drovers. After about 3½ miles the road plummets down a short, steep descent, quickly followed by a short, steep uphill. On reaching the top you will see a turn off to the right (signposted Pateley Bridge/Steep Hill). **Turn R** here and this road will take you back to where you began. *Don't worry – the 'steep hill' is actually*

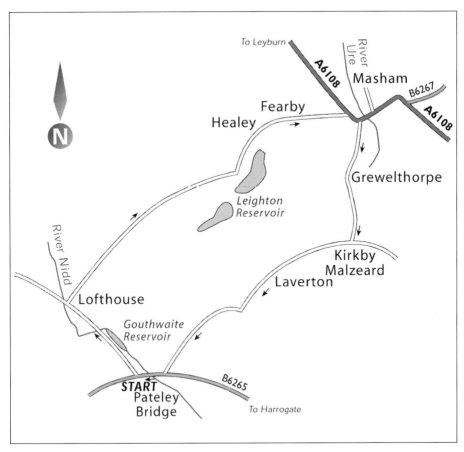

downhill into Pateley Bridge, but please be extremely careful on the descent as it is 1:5 (20%) in parts. On reaching the T-junction at the bottom of the hill, **turn R** onto the main street and the car park is on your **L** just after the bridge that crosses the River Nidd.

PATELEY BRIDGE

Pateley Bridge is the capital of Nidderdale and an ancient crossing place over the River Nidd, though the present bridge dates from the 18th century. The town is made up of mostly 18th and 19th century stone buildings, but also contains the oldest sweet shop in England, dated to 1661 – you'll find it on the main street. There are magnificent views from the Panorama Walk above the town.

HOW STEAN GORGE

The spectacular limestone gorge is up to 80 ft deep in places and is a popular tourist attraction. The gorge is accessible via a narrow footpath. There is an entrance fee, and mountain bike hire is available.

MASHAM

This small market town lies beside the River Ure, on the A6108. As well as a number of shops, galleries and stone cottages, Masham also contains two breweries – Theakston's and Black Sheep.

The café at How Stean Gorge

6

Kirkby Stephen: Tan Hill Circuit

25 miles

The Tan Hill Inn is the highest pub in Britain, at 1,732 ft above sea level. Here, there is nothing for miles around and on a clear day, the views extend far into County Durham and beyond. The first half of this ride is uphill for much of the way, but what goes up must come down and you then descend through Kaber back to the little market town of Kirkby Stephen.

Map: OS Landranger 91 Appleby-in-Westmorland (GR 775087).

Starting point: The free car park at the northern side of Kirkby Stephen, very close to the livestock sale area and well signposted from the town centre.

Refreshments: There are several cafés and pubs in Kirkby Stephen, and the pub at Nateby and the Tan Hill Inn serve food.

The route: Very hilly all the way round, with the 12-mile stretch from Nateby to the Tan Hill Inn uphill most of the way.

Turn R out of the car park and continue to a T-junction with a mini roundabout, where **turn R** into the town centre. On reaching the traffic lights, **turn L** (signposted Nateby/Hawes) onto the B6259. Continue to Nateby and on reaching the junction opposite the Black Bull Inn, **turn L** onto the B6270 (signposted Swaledale/Reeth).

The ride now follows the B6270 for the next 8½ miles, climbing to nearly 1,800 ft above sea level on Birkdale Common. Some of the gradients are steep so you may have to walk a few of them, but be careful as there is no pavement! It is a steady climb for the first 3 miles that steepens towards the top, which is when you enter North Yorkshire and commence your descent towards Keld.

After 8½ miles on this road, **turn L** onto a minor road (signposted W. Stonedale/Tan Hill). This stretch takes you to the

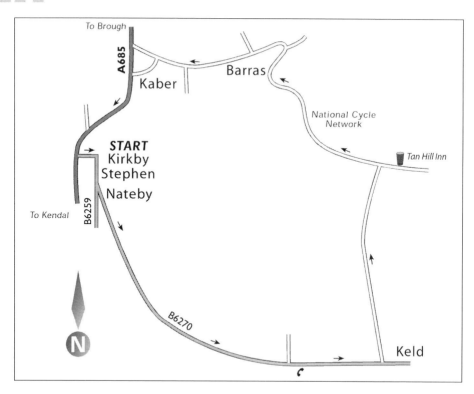

The highest pub in Britain

Tan Hill Inn. The road is hilly in parts, eventually arriving at a T-junction. *If you wish,* **turn R** *to visit the pub.*

Otherwise, **turn L** (signposted Kaber). This road forms part of the National Cycle Network. You will now be rewarded for all your hard work as the road descends towards Kaber. After 5½ miles, at a T-junction **turn L** (signposted Kaber/Kirkby Stephen). Continue on this minor road for 4 miles, passing through Kaber village. At the T-junction with the A685, **turn L** (signposted Keld/Kirkby Stephen) and follow this road back to Kirkby Stephen.

● ●

KIRKBY STEPHEN

Kirkby Stephen lies at the head of the Eden Valley. The church of St Stephen dates originally from Saxon times but was rebuilt in 1220 and has a 16th century tower. Between the church and the market square stands the Cloisters, which served for a long time as a butter market. Surrounding the market square is an ancient collar of cobblestones which marked out an area used for bull baiting, a sport that ceased here in 1820 after a bull broke loose, causing mayhem.

KELD

One of the smallest villages in Yorkshire, Keld derives its name from the Norse, meaning 'spring' or 'well'. The Pennine Way passes through here on its way to Tan Hill. One interesting feature is the chapel with its sundial.

The sundial on the wall of Keld chapel

(**7**)

Richmond: The Stang Round

31 miles

A hilly start to this ride taking in the extreme north of the county, with great views, as you climb up over The Stang. The route then crosses over into County Durham before returning to Richmond and its 11th century castle along undulating country lanes, passing through attractive little villages on the way.

Maps: OS Landranger 92 Barnard Castle and 98 Wensleydale and Upper Wharfedale (GR 169008).

Starting point: The market square in Richmond town centre, which is also a car park.

Refreshments: There are several cafés and pubs in Richmond. En route, there is a café in Reeth and pubs in most of the villages, serving food.

The route: Very hilly in the first half, though after you turn to head back to Richmond the terrain is varied but not difficult. This is a long route and you may want to take advantage of refreshments before you start.

Leave the market square via King Street (signposted Tourist Information Centre) and on reaching the roundabout, take the **first exit** (signposted Reeth/Leyburn). Proceed as far as the petrol station, where **turn R** onto Hurgill Road (signposted Long Stay Parking). The ride now follows this country road for the next few miles. It's a flattish ride to begin with but after about 3 miles, the road descends so be careful, and about 1 mile later you will pass through the village of Marske.

Continue through Marske, follow the road round to the left and descend to the bottom of the hill, where **turn R** at a T-junction (signposted Marrick/Hurst/Reeth) and engage lowest gear to climb the hill out of the village. Follow this undulating road for the next 4 miles as far as a T-junction in

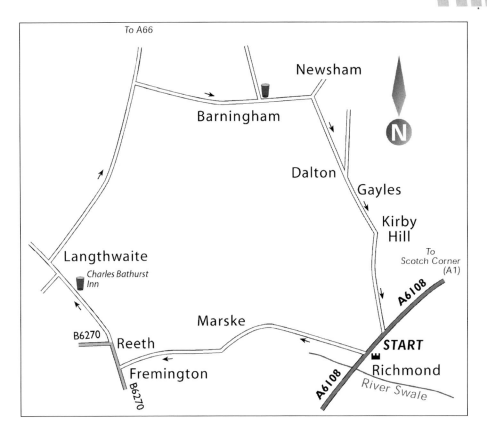

the village of Fremington, where **turn R** onto the B6270 (signposted Reeth) and continue to Reeth village.

On arriving at the junction beside the Buck Hotel, **turn R** onto a minor road (signposted Langthwaite/Barnard Castle) and continue for 3 miles or so. At Langthwaite, carry on through the village and at the junction about 100 yards beyond the Charles Bathurst Inn, **turn R** (signposted Barnard Castle), descend over the bridge and then

engage lowest gear to climb the hill out of the village.

The ride now follows this minor road for the next 5½ miles. It is a steep climb to begin with, before the ascent becomes more gradual and lasts about 2½ miles as far as the County Durham border, at which point you'll begin your welcome descent! The complete descent lasts about 3 miles and is narrow in places, so be careful.

Shortly after passing a postbox and telephone kiosk in quick succession, **turn R** (signposted Barningham/Scargill). The ride becomes much easier now but the terrain is still rolling, much of it through open countryside. Continue for the next 5 miles, passing through Barningham village to Newsham. On reaching the second set of crossroads beside the memorial and telephone box, **turn R** (signposted Dalton/Gayles). Continue for another ½ mile, follow the road round to the right (signposted Dalton/Gayles) and continue to Dalton, where **turn R** at the T-junction (signposted Gayles/Kirby Hill/Richmond). At the junction beside the Travellers Rest pub, **turn L** (signposted Richmond).

Now continue through Gayles and Kirby Hill and you'll eventually arrive at a T-junction, where **turn R**. This road takes you directly back to Richmond. It is an undulating ride for the 3½ mile journey, culminating with a descent to a T-junction (A6108) with a set of traffic lights. **Turn R** (signposted Richmond/Reeth) and continue to the roundabout, where take the first exit (signposted Town Centre/Catterick Garrison) to return to the market place.

RICHMOND
Richmond Castle dates back to 1071, when the original was built by Alan Rufus, reaching its final form in the 14th century. Two road

The attractive pub in Langthwaite passed on the route

Richmond Castle

bridges cross the River Swale in the town. The older of the two, Green Bridge, was erected in 1789 after the existing bridge was swept away by water. Also in the town, in the market square, is the Green Howards Museum, the regimental museum of the North Ridings Infantry, based in the old Trinity church. The regiment itself dates back to 1688. Also nearby, on the wall of a house near to where you turn right into Hurgill Road, is a plaque dedicated to the total eclipse of the sun, of which the centre line of the path of totality crossed over the town on 29th June 1927.

LANGTHWAITE
Langthwaite is Arkengarthdale's largest village, lying about 3 miles north-west of Reeth. The pub is named after Charles Bathurst, who was an 18th century lord of the manor.

8

Richmond: Jervaulx Abbey

29 miles

ervaulx Abbey is one of the Yorkshire Dales' most popular attractions, a 12th century abbey set in beautiful countryside to the south-west of Richmond. This route begins with a level ride out through the military town of Catterick Garrison and after passing through the delightfully named Newton le Willows, you have the opportunity to visit the abbey – and perhaps its tearooms! After this it is a splendid ride through the market towns of Middleham and Leyburn, some of which uses A-roads, until a country road takes you back to Richmond, with fine views of the castle.

Maps: OS Landranger 92 Barnard Castle and 99 Northallerton and Ripon (GR 169008).

Starting point: Richmond market square, where there is car parking.

Refreshments: Richmond has several cafés and pubs and there are pubs serving food in most of the villages en route. There is a tearoom at Jervaulx Abbey, and you will also find cafés at Middleham and Leyburn.

The route: The terrain is varied but not too difficult, although you should take extra care while passing through Catterick Garrison and be aware of the possibility of military vehicles in this area.

Leave Richmond market square via New Road and continue to a T-junction, where **turn L** and descend to the bridge. Cross over the bridge and engage lowest gear to climb the short steep hill. At the top, **turn L** (signposted Catterick Garrison) and continue to a T-junction, where **turn R** to enter Catterick Garrison. Continue to the first roundabout and take the **second exit** (signposted Town Centre/A6136). Continue to traffic lights beside McDonalds, where continue straight on to the next roundabout. Go straight on onto Scotton Road (signposted

Scotton), continue to the next roundabout and go straight on again onto a minor road (signposted Scotton/Patrick Brompton).

Continue to Scotton. The ride now follows this minor road for the next 3½ miles (Bedale Road), following signposts for Bedale/Masham, as far as the crossroads with the A684. Go straight over (signposted Newton le Willows/Masham) and continue to Newton le Willows village.

On arriving at the crossroads beside the postbox, **turn R** onto Station Road. Continue for 2 miles, passing Aysgarth School, to a T-junction, where **turn L** (signposted Bedale). At the junction opposite Cocked Hat Farm, **turn R** (signposted Jervaulx/Masham). Proceed to the crossroads, where continue straight on (no signpost) until you reach a T-junction with the A6108. **Turn R** (signposted Middleham/Leyburn). Take care on this road at all times as this is the main road linking

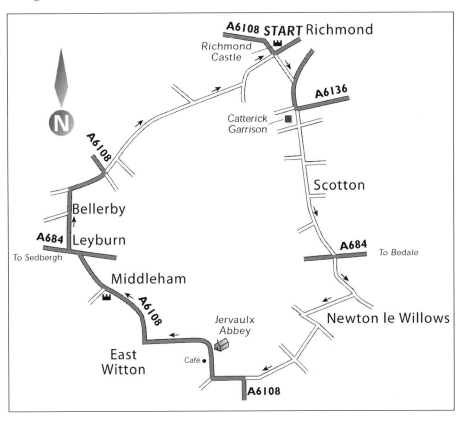

Jervaulx Abbey

Wensleydale and Ripon so it can get busy at times. Continue for about 1 mile.

*If you require refreshments, **turn L** into the car park (signposted Jervaulx Abbey/tearoom) and you will see the tearoom ahead of you.*

Continue on the A6108 and on reaching East Witton village, follow the road round to the right (signposted Leyburn/A6108) and continue for a further 2 miles to Middleham. Where the road divides beside the memorial, follow the road round to the right

(signposted Leyburn) and continue for a further 2 miles. At a T-junction in Leyburn, **turn L** (signposted Hawes/Richmond) and continue to the main market place.

On reaching the T-junction and mini-roundabout, **turn R** (signposted Bellerby/Catterick Camp/Richmond) to remain on the A6108. In about ½ mile you will come to a mini-roundabout, where go straight on and continue for a further 2 miles, passing through Bellerby village. You eventually arrive at a

T-junction, where **turn R** (signposted Catterick Camp/Reeth/Richmond). In ¾ mile you will arrive at another road junction.

You can take the A6108 back to Richmond if you wish, but I recommend a detour. Do not follow the road round to the left, but go straight on onto a minor road (signposted Catterick Camp). Ascend a short hill and **fork L** on the right-hand bend (signposted Byway – it is a brown sign and the slip road is easy to miss!). This road leads directly to Richmond. It is a 5-mile journey back to the starting point and on

your descent into the town you will have a splendid view of Richmond Castle.

LEYBURN

Leyburn received its market charter in 1684. Market day is Friday and that's when the town is at its busiest. The streets are lined with late Georgian and Victorian stone buildings and every year, usually around the beginning of May, the town hosts the Dales Festival of Food and Drink. Leyburn Shawl, to the west of the town, is a mile-long limestone scarp offering panoramic views of Wensleydale, and it's rumoured that it got its name when

Seen on a wall in Richmond (see page 39)

Mary, Queen of Scots dropped her shawl here during her unsuccessful escape attempt from nearby Bolton Castle! More recently, in 2003 the Yorkshire Dales saw the reopening of the old Wensleydale Railway between the National Park and Leeming Bar, now offering regular service operated through a private company.

JERVAULX ABBEY

Jervaulx Abbey was founded in 1156 and was home to monks of the Cistercian Order for almost four centuries, until the abbey fell victim to Henry VIII during the Dissolution of the Monasteries. Today this fascinating site, which is open to the public every day, is privately owned but supported by English Heritage.

MIDDLEHAM

Middleham is situated about 2 miles south of Leyburn. The castle was built in about 1170 by Robert Fitz Randolph, during the reign of Henry II. As a young prince, the future Richard III was sent here at the age of 13 to be trained in the 'arts of nobilitie', and he was very popular locally.

(**9**)

Tan Hill and Swaledale

26 miles

A very scenic circuit of the northern Dales with the opportunity of visiting the Tan Hill Inn, the highest pub in England. The opening 11 miles through Arkengarthdale show off the rugged landscape at its best, with views for miles over open countryside at Tan Hill. After a descent to Thwaite, the ride returns to the flatter lands of Swaledale, passing through pretty little villages – including Keld, where the chapel and its sundial are worth a small detour – and over a haunted bridge on the way back to Reeth.

Maps: OS Landranger 98 Wensleydale and Upper Wharfedale and 92 Barnard Castle (GR 038993)

Starting point: Reeth village green, where there is a pay-and-display car park.

Refreshments: Several cafés surround the village green at Reeth. En route, the Charles Bathurst Inn just after Langthwaite village serves food but after this there is nothing until the Tan Hill Inn. Then refreshments are available in virtually every village along the B6270 between Thwaite and Reeth, including the Kearton Tea Shop at Thwaite.

The route: The first 3 miles or so are relatively flat before climbing over Arkengarthdale to the Tan Hill Inn; this country lane forms part of the National Cycle Network. After the inn, it's a gradual descent to Keld before the flatter roads of Swaledale.

On leaving Reeth village green, take the minor road (signposted Langthwaite/Barnard Castle). The first 3 miles to Langthwaite are relatively straightforward and shortly after passing through the village you will see the Charles Bathurst Inn on your right-hand side. The route now follows a quiet road through rugged countryside, much of it uphill! The loneliness of the area becomes more apparent the nearer the Tan Hill Inn you get and you can see for miles around over the open moorland, which

Keld chapel

stretches far away to the horizon. You pass the Tan Hill Inn on the right-hand side, before arriving at a junction.

At the junction, **turn L** (signposted Keld/Thwaite). It is a 3¾ mile ride along this country lane, much of which is downhill and will be a welcome relief after that tough section. Take extra care when descending to the B6270 T-junction, as the road is very steep. On arriving at the T-junction, **turn L** (signposted Keld/Reeth/Richmond). This road will eventually lead you back to

Reeth, passing through a string of picturesque villages, the first of which is Keld.

It is worth leaving the main route to see the chapel and its sundial. **Turn L** *(signposted Keld Only) and* **turn L** *again at the bottom of the hill, where you'll see the chapel in front of you. Come back to the main route when ready.*

Continue on the B6270 and the next village you will arrive at is Thwaite, where the Kearton Tea Shop is on your left as you descend through the village.

Continue on the B6270, cross over the bridge and about 1 mile after the turn-off for Buttertubs Pass you will arrive at Muker. There is a tearoom just before the church on your left-hand side. Carry straight on and a further 3 miles down the road you cross over a bridge (said to be haunted!) into Gunnerside, Swaledale's largest village. A mile further on is Low Row, quickly followed by Feetham – the pubs in both these villages serve food.

Healaugh, a further 1 mile on, is the final village before arriving back at Reeth.

REETH

Reeth is seen by many as the capital of Upper Swaledale. Most of the buildings date back to the 18th and 19th centuries and the village is home to the Swaledale Folk Museum, which is housed in what was once the old Methodist Sunday School.

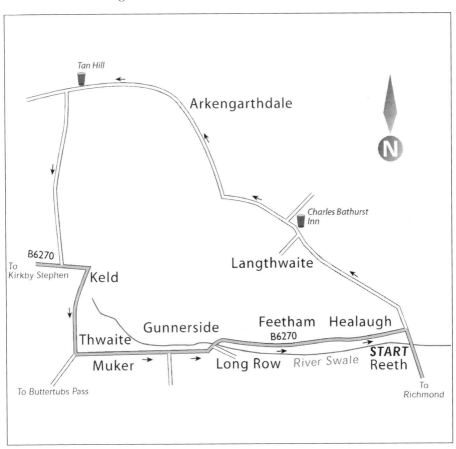

One of the many refreshment stops available – this one in Thwaite

GUNNERSIDE

Gunnerside derives its name from the Norse for 'Gunner's pasture', Gunner being a hero in Norse mythology. The Yorkshire writer Thomas Armstrong lived nearby and set his novel *Adam Brunskill* within this community, which until the 19th century was very much a lead-mining village. This is evident at the village tearooms, where you can sample such delights as Lead Mines Bait and Gunnerside Cheesecake, made from old recipes from mining days. The bridge that you cross on your entry to the village is reputed to be haunted by a headless ghost.

10

Coverdale and Park Rash

31 miles

A quite hilly ride through wonderful countryside, which takes you over the hills of Coverdale to descend the very steep hairpin-road known as Park Rash to the attractive village of Kettlewell. Then the route continues into Wensleydale and over Kidstones Pass to Bishopdale, enjoying the waterfalls on the surrounding cliffs, before returning to Aysgarth Falls.

Maps: OS Landranger 98 Wensleydale and Upper Wharfedale and 99 Northallerton and Ripon (GR 012884).

Starting point: The main coach park near Aysgarth Falls, which is also a pay-and-display car park.

Refreshments: Aysgarth has a café on its main street. En route, there are cafés in West Witton and Kettlewell that welcome cyclists, as well as pubs in Carlton, Starbotton, Buckden and Cray that serve food.

The route: The first 20 miles are hilly, with a long sloping climb up Coverdale, a 1:4 (25%) descent into Kettlewell, and a short steep climb over Kidstones. After that descent there is a 5-mile ride on the flatter roads of Bishopdale before the final climb from Thoralby.

Turn L out of the Aysgarth Falls car park and on reaching the T-junction with the A684, **turn L** (signposted West Witton/Leyburn/Bedale). Proceed on the A684 until you reach West Witton village, where **turn R** onto a minor road (signposted Melmerby/Carlton). Continue for about 1 mile and where the road divides, **fork R** (signposted Melmerby/Carlton). Continue to the T-junction in Melmerby, where **turn R** (no signpost). Continue for about ½ mile to another T-junction, where **turn R** (signposted Carlton/Horsehouse/Kettlewell). This is part of the National Cycle Network (Route 65).

The ride now follows this minor

The dramatic Aysgarth Falls

road for the next 11 miles all the way to Kettlewell. It's rolling to begin with but sometime after Coverham the road tilts upwards and climbs over an area known as Coverdale. It is a gradual ascent and on reaching the top, it's then a very steep descent known as Park Rash towards Kettlewell.

Continue to the T-junction, where **turn R** (signposted Buckden/Aysgarth) and on reaching the T-junction with the B6160 opposite the Racehorses pub, **turn R**. The ride now follows the B6160 for the next 12 miles through an area known as Wharfedale. It is mainly flat for about 5 miles with a few inclines and declines before climbing over the Kidstones Pass and on into Bishopdale. On the ascent, you will have the chance to enjoy the surrounding waterfalls but the road is steep at times so you may be reduced to walking! At the top you will be rewarded for all your efforts with a descent into Bishopdale, after which the ride takes to flatter roads.

Continue for a further 5 miles and eventually you will arrive at the village of West Burton, where follow the road around to the left (signposted Aysgarth/Hawes). **Turn L** here and engage lowest gear to climb the short steep hill up to the T-junction with the A684. **Turn L** (signposted Aysgarth/Hawes) to return to Aysgarth village.

. . . .

AYSGARTH

Aysgarth Falls are amongst Yorkshire's most popular attractions and are easily seen from the bridge that crosses the River Ure. The church of St Andrew dates back to

1866 and its four-acre churchyard is the largest in England.

KETTLEWELL

Kettlewell is very popular with tourists. Most of the cottages surrounding the village date to the 17th and 18th centuries. St Mary's church dates to the 18th century but the churchyard and lychgate stand on the site of a 12th century building. A market was established in the 13th century and the village later became a thriving community. During the late 1700s and early 1800s, textiles and lead mining revitalised Kettlewell after the

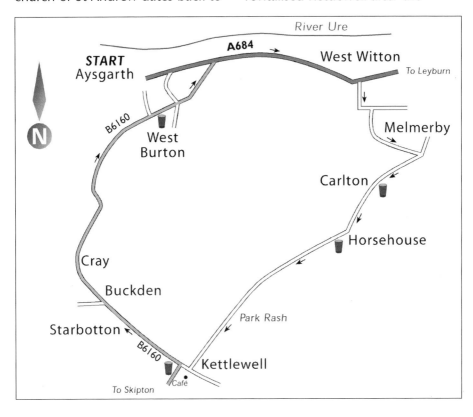

village had declined throughout the early 17th century. More recently, it was the setting for the acclaimed film *Calendar Girls*. There are no fewer than three pubs in the village and the Cottage Tearoom welcomes cyclists so there are no problems finding refreshments here!

BUCKDEN
Buckden derives its name from 'valley of the bucks' and the village is overlooked by Buckden Pike. On top of the hill stands a memorial to the Polish crew of an aircraft that crashed here in 1942, from which only one person survived. The village also hosts its own annual fell race over Buckden Pike. The race is 4 miles long and finishes on the gala field.

WEST BURTON
Grey and brown stone cottages and houses surround the rectangular green within this small village situated just off the B6160 Bishopdale road. In the centre you will find a stepped market cross that was erected in 1820 and remembers the times when a large weekly market or fair was held on the green.

11
Swaledale and Castle Bolton
23 miles

The hills that divide Swaledale, with its buttercup meadows and picturesque villages, and Wensleydale, with its waterfalls and market towns, are the focus of this ride. After a flat start, the route climbs over Summer Lodge Moor to Reeth, home of the Swaledale Folk Museum. Then comes a climb over Harkerside Moor, before returning to the famous Aysgarth Falls through Castle Bolton, where there is the chance to stop and explore the ancient castle.

Maps: OS Landranger 98 Wensleydale and Upper Wharfedale (GR 012884).

Starting point: Aysgarth Falls pay-and-display car park (the main coach park near the falls).

Refreshments: There are at least two cafés in Aysgarth, and en route you will find cafés in Askrigg and Reeth, as well as at the castle in Castle Bolton.

The route: There are two major climbs on the ride, between Askrigg and Healaugh and between Reeth and Castle Bolton. However, the last 5 miles back from Carperby are rolling but nothing too strenuous.

Turn R out of the car park and continue to the T-junction in Carperby, where **turn L** (signposted Askrigg/Hawes). In 3½ miles, **turn R** (signposted Newbiggin) and after ½ mile, where the road divides at the grass triangle, **turn R** (no signpost, so easy to miss). Engage lowest gear to climb the hill.

The ride now climbs over Summer Lodge Moor into Swaledale for the next 5 miles, much of which is downhill after the initial climb. **Turn L** (signposted Reeth), continue over the bridge and on reaching the T-junction, **turn R** (no signpost but it's the B6270). Continue to Reeth, where there are cafés if you require refreshments.

Continue on the B6270 through Reeth and Fremington to Grinton (signposted Leyburn/Richmond). On reaching the junction beside Jennings Bridge Inn, go straight ahead (signposted Redmire/Leyburn) onto a minor road. Engage lowest gear to climb the hill out of the village and where the road divides just after the cattle grid, **turn R** (signposted Redmire) and continue over the hill.

In about 4 miles, on the descent towards Redmire, **turn R** (signposted Castle Bolton) and continue to the T-junction opposite the castle. There is a café inside the castle if you would like to stop. Otherwise, **turn L** (signposted Carperby/ Aysgarth/Redmire) and descend to a T-junction, where **turn R** (signposted Carperby/Aysgarth Falls/ Askrigg). Continue to Carperby and on reaching the junction shortly after the memorial, **turn L** (signposted Aysgarth Falls/National Park Centre) and retrace your route to the car park. You will be able to see the falls from the bridge on your entry into Aysgarth village.

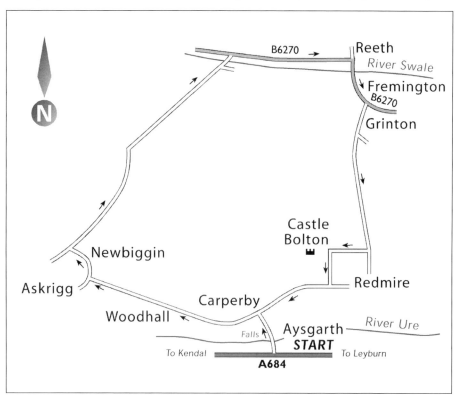

The imposing Castle Bolton is well worth a visit

REETH

This is the largest village in Swaledale and once had a flourishing weekly market and fair. Now many people come to visit the Swaledale Folk Museum in the old school, which has displays and information on life in the dale over the centuries; it is open Thursday, Friday and Sunday through the summer.

GRINTON

Just a mile south of Reeth lies this quiet little village. The church of St Andrew dates from the 13th and 15th centuries, though there are still some Norman remains.

BOLTON CASTLE

Dominating the skyline looking north from Wensleydale, Bolton Castle, with its 9-ft thick walls, was built in 1379 by Lord Richard Scrope, treasurer and chancellor to Richard II. Mary, Queen of Scots was imprisoned here for a time before attempting to escape in 1569 – she lost her shawl while crossing the moors, which led to her recapture. During the Civil War, the castle was besieged for over a year by Cromwell's troops, eventually surrendering in 1645, after which it was partially dismantled. The north-east tower fell during a storm in 1761. The castle is open to the public.

12

Langstrothdale and Fleet Moss

31 miles

A scenic circuit of the Yorkshire Dales that takes in some of the most spectacular sights in the county. The ride begins with a flattish section through Wensleydale, passing through pretty villages such as Askrigg, where *All Creatures Great and Small* was filmed. After Aysgarth Falls, the route follows the valley of Bishopdale before climbing over Kidstones into Wharfedale, with its picturesque villages and hamlets. After passing through Langstrothdale alongside the River Wharfe, the ride returns to Hawes over Fleet Moss, the highest road in Yorkshire, with an equally rewarding descent to Gayle on the way back to Hawes.

Map: OS Landranger 98 Wensleydale and Upper Wharfedale (GR 870897).

Starting point: There are several car parks at Hawes, but the ride directions start from the one at the Wensleydale Creamery pay-and-display.

Refreshments: Hawes has several cafés that welcome cyclists. En route, there are cafés at Askrigg, Carperby and Aysgarth, while Cray and Hubberholme both have country pubs serving food. I recommend that you take advantage of these before tackling Fleet Moss.

The route: The terrain is varied and is split into two parts – the first 15 miles or so to the foot of Kidstones are undulating, before the two major climbs over Kidstones Pass and Fleet Moss.

Turn R out of the Creamery car park and on reaching the T-junction with the A684, **turn R** into Hawes town centre. Continue for about ½ mile, then **turn L** onto a minor road (signposted Muker/Hardraw). On reaching a T-junction, **turn R** (signposted Sedbusk).

The ride now follows a minor road for the next 4½ miles to Askrigg. Continue through the village and where the road divides beside the Crown Inn, **fork R** (signposted Carperby/Leyburn). Continue for a further 4 miles and, before you reach Carperby, **turn R** (signposted Aysgarth Falls/National Park Centre). It's about 1 mile to the village, during which time you will pass over a bridge where you have a view of Aysgarth Falls, before climbing steeply to a T-junction with the A684.

Turn L (signposted West Witton/Leyburn/Bedale) and in about 200 yards, **turn R** onto a minor road (signposted West Burton/Kettlewell). Continue to a T-junction with the B6160, where **turn R** (signposted Kettlewell/Skipton). The ride now follows the B6160 for the next 8 miles, climbing over a steep hill known as Kidstones. On arriving at the top of the hill, the road is flat for about 1 mile before it eventually descends into the village of Cray. There are waterfalls all around you! As you continue your descent into Wharfedale, **turn R** on a minor

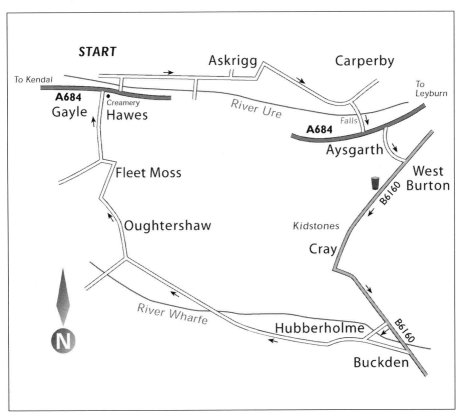

road (signposted Hubberholme) and continue until you reach a T-junction, where **turn R**. This road takes you directly back to Hawes.

After 2 miles you pass over a bridge, shortly after which you commence your ascent over Fleet Moss, the highest road in Yorkshire. Continue for a further 3 miles, follow the road round to the right (signposted Hawes) and engage lowest gear to climb the short, steep hill. You've then got the chance for a breather as the road descends into the village of

Oughtershaw before commencing your final ascent to Fleet Moss, where there is a parking area for a final breather before the long, steep descent back to Hawes, passing through Gayle village on the way.

ASKRIGG

This small village just off the A684 near Bainbridge is a popular spot, as it was the setting for the television series *All Creatures Great and Small*. Visitors will recognise Cringle House as the vets' surgery, Skeldale House. The church of St

The road into Hawes

The Creamery where the ride begins

Oswald, in the centre of the village, dates back to the 15th century.

CRAY

A small village surrounded by waterfalls, just north of Buckden on the B6160, it consists mainly of farm buildings and stone cottages, many of which were built between 1750 and 1850. The White Lion is the highest pub in Wharfedale.

HUBBERHOLME

Hubberholme is a very small village sitting at the foot of Langstrothdale. Each year, on New Year's Day, the village locals gather at the pub, the George Inn. An auction then takes place for the rent of the field behind the church and the highest bidder gains the lease for a year. St Michael's church was once so badly flooded that fish were seen swimming in the nave – well, it might be a myth, but it's an interesting story!

(13)

Hawes and Buttertubs Pass

19 miles

Allow plenty of time for this ride, which covers an area of breathtaking scenery but includes two of the steepest hills in the county! The climbing starts almost immediately over the Buttertubs Pass, at almost 1,800 ft above sea level, into Swaledale. After passing through Muker, the home of Swaledale Woollens, the route then climbs over Askrigg Common, following the Yorkshire Cycle Way on the return to Hawes in Wensleydale, on rolling country roads.

Map: OS Landranger 98 Wensleydale and Upper Wharfedale (GR 870897).

Starting point: The Wensleydale Creamery car park (pay-and-display) at Hawes.

Refreshments: There are several cafés in Hawes, Thwaite and Muker each have a tearoom, and there are also cafés at Askrigg and Bainbridge, the latter just off the route.

The route: The first 5 miles are virtually all uphill as you climb over the Buttertubs Pass. After passing through Swaledale, there is another stiff climb over to Askrigg.

Turn R out of the car park and on reaching the T-junction, **turn R** into Hawes town centre. Continue through Hawes (the road becomes one-way) for about ½ mile, and **turn L** onto a minor road (signposted Hardraw/ Muker). Continue for ¾ mile and **turn L** at the T-junction, and in 100 yards, **turn R** (signposted Muker via Buttertubs Pass).

The climb begins with an incline through Simonstone village, followed by a couple of steep sections that you might have to walk. The gradient eases after the first cattle grid and after the second cattle grid, about 1 mile further on, you'll undergo a 2-mile descent into Swaledale, which is 1:4 (25%) in places so be careful, especially on the hair-pin bends, eventually arriving at a T-junction. *If you require refreshments,* **turn L**, *cycle over the bridge and shortly you'll see the Kearton Tea Shop on your right.*

For the main route, **turn R** at the T-junction with the B6270 (signposted Muker/Richmond) and continue to Muker village, where there is another tearoom. After a further mile along the B6270, **turn R** onto a minor road (signposted Askrigg) and engage lowest gear to climb the 1:4 (25%) hill. If you can't manage the hill, then walk the first part. This is a 2½ mile gradual ascent that eases the higher you climb.

After the cattle grid you can enjoy the 2-mile descent into Askrigg village. On reaching the T-junction, **turn R** (signposted Hawes) and continue through the village. In 1 mile, **fork R** where the road divides (signposted Hardraw). The ride now follows a rolling country lane through

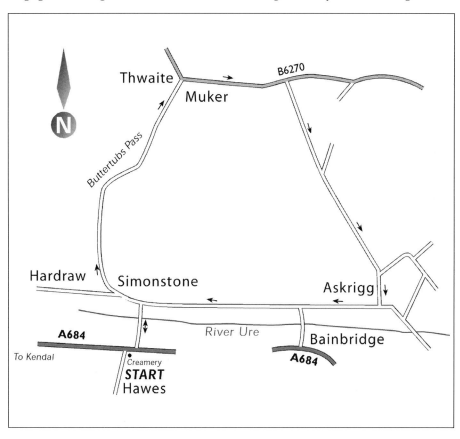

Wensleydale. After 3½ miles, **turn L** (signposted Hawes/C32) and continue to a T-junction. **Turn R** (signposted Sedbergh/Ingleton) and retrace your route back to Hawes.

• •

BUTTERTUBS PASS

The 1,726 ft high road that runs through the Pass is one of the most scenic roads in the country, linking Wensleydale and Swaledale. The Buttertubs themselves are a curious natural feature of stone stacks that are up to 90 ft deep in places, and it is said that farmers would lower their unsold butter into the tubs in order to keep it cool while on the way home from Hawes market.

THWAITE

The name Thwaite is derived from the Nordic language, meaning a clearing in the wood. The village was nearly washed away during a great flood towards the end of the 19th century. Richard and Cherry Kearton, pioneers of natural wildlife photography, were born here and the village tearooms are named after them – their initials can be found carved on nearby Keartons Cottage to commemorate their birthplace.

MUKER

The village of Muker is 1 mile east of Thwaite on the B6270. The church of St Mary dates to the 16th century, although it has been

The picturesque village of Muker

A welcome seat on the Muker road

altered over the centuries. As well as the church, the village comprises a chapel, an institute, greystone cottages and shops – and Swaledale Woollens. The local Swaledale sheep provided the wool and knitting supplemented the income of many families during the days when lead mining employed most of the villagers. Now it is a cottage industry in its own right.

14
Widdale and Shaking Moss
23 miles

outh-west of Hawes is the area known as Widdale and this challenging ride passes over Newby Head into Dentdale, with Ingleborough on the horizon before straying for a while into Cumbria. The route then tackles the climb to Galloway Gate and passes Dent railway station, the highest mainline station in England. The viaduct of the Settle to Carlisle Railway is an outstanding landmark in the area. Shaking Moss is popular with cyclists, and after the descent to Garsdale Head, the ride follows the main road back to Hawes, but not before a chance to visit the lovely Hardraw Force waterfall.

Map: OS Landranger 98 Wensleydale and Upper Wharfedale (GR: 870897).

Starting point: The Wensleydale Creamery car park in Hawes (pay-and-display).

Refreshments: As well as cafés in Hawes, the pub in Dentdale serves food, as does the Moorcock Inn at Garsdale Head. The village of Hardraw has a tearoom and the Green Dragon inn.

The route: The climbs out of Hawes and Cowgill require exceptionally low gears, but the A684 is rolling but not difficult.

Turn R out of the car park and proceed to the T-junction with the A684 in Hawes. **Turn L** and where the road divides, **fork L** (signposted Ingleton) onto the B6255 and engage lowest gear to climb the hill out of the village. The ride now follows the B6255 for the next 7 miles, climbing over Newby Head. It is a gradual ascent with some downhill bits so it's not a continuous haul and the last mile to where you turn off for Dentdale is mainly downhill.

After 7 miles **turn R** onto a minor road (signposted Dent/Sedbergh). The ride now follows this minor road for the next 3½ miles, entering Cumbria just after the junction. Shortly after, there is a long downhill section under the viaduct of the Settle to Carlisle Railway and through the village of Cowgill. Continue past the Sportsman's Inn and at the junction beside the red telephone box, **turn R** (signposted Dent Station/Garsdale Head) and engage lowest gear to climb the hill. You are now climbing over Shaking Moss, a route popular with cyclists, although after the initial steep section it's downhill for much of the way. Continue for the 4¾ miles to Garsdale Head and at the T-junction with the A684, **turn R** (signposted Hawes).

You can ride all the way back to Hawes on the A684 if you wish, but I recommend a detour to Hardraw Force. After about 5 miles, just before a road bridge over the River Ure, **turn L** (signposted Hardraw) onto a minor road and continue to Hardraw village. *To view Hardraw Force, enter through the Green Dragon inn, where you will have to pay a small fee; take the path of about ½ mile to the waterfall (it's possible to cycle on it!).* To continue on the main route, go on through Hardraw village and **turn R** (signposted Hawes) to continue to the T-junction with the A684 in

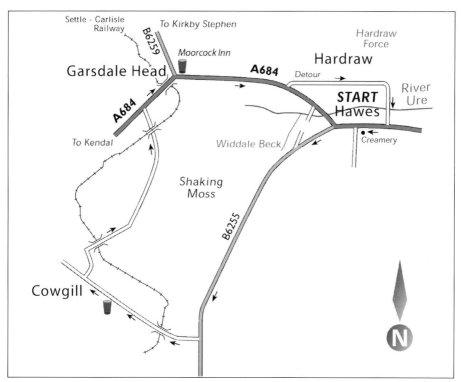

Hawes. **Turn R** to return to the Wensleydale Creamery.

⬤ ⬤

HAWES

Hawes derives its name from hals, a Norse word meaning a neck. At 850 ft above sea level, it is the highest market town in England, having been granted its charter in 1699. Many of the buildings date from Victorian times, though some survive from the 18th century. The old railway station now houses the Dales Countryside Museum and National Park Centre. Outside there is a length of track and the old station platform. The museum is

The spectacular Hardraw Force

The pub at Garsdale Head

open daily throughout the summer months, with limited opening in winter.

SETTLE-CARLISLE RAILWAY

Settle is, of course, the starting point for the famous Settle-Carlisle Railway. The line passes through 14 tunnels and over 21 viaducts as well as numerous bridges on its 72-mile journey through Yorkshire and Cumbria. It was the last railway line in England to be built with the aid of horse and cart! It opened in 1876 and contains the highest mainline station in England at Dent. Shortly after this, the line reaches its highest point of 1,169 ft at Aisgill, which is between Garsdale and Kirkby Stephen, although the gradient never exceeds 1:100.

HARDRAW

Only 1½ miles from Hawes is the village of Hardraw. The entrance to the grounds of Hardraw Force is through the Green Dragon pub, with a path to the waterfall, Hardraw Force. The 100 ft drop of water is the longest single drop in England. It is a popular tourist destination and has been so for a long time – William Wordsworth visited here in December 1799 with his sister Dorothy, and the landscape artist John Turner painted the Force.

15

Pen-y-Ghent and Littondale

26 miles

This is a hilly ride around Malhamdale and Darnbrook with breathtaking views across to Pen-y-ghent, Ingleborough and Malham Tarn. After the descent into Halton Gill, the route takes to the flatter roads of Littondale where you arrive at Arncliffe, a picturesque little village that was the setting for early episodes of the television soap opera *Emmerdale Farm*. Then you return to the hills of Malham Moor, which is a fine example of the rugged landscape of the Dales. The route criss-crosses the Pennine Way on a number of occasions but you'll encounter far more sheep than people whilst passing over Darnbrook Fell, before the return to Settle and a tricky descent into Langcliffe that presents the limestone crags at their best.

Map: OS Landranger 98 Wensleydale and Upper Wharfedale (GR 818639).

Starting point: Settle coach park, which also serves as a 24-hour car park (pay-and-display).

Refreshments: In Settle you will be spoilt for choice, with Poppies Tearoom and the Settle Down and Naked Man cafés, as well as a range of inns. En route, there are pubs at Langcliffe, Stainforth, Litton and Arncliffe, all serving food. Arncliffe also has a tearoom.

The route: This is one of the more difficult rides. You will need plenty of time to complete the route and low gears will be an asset on the climbs out of Stainforth and Arncliffe.

On leaving the car park, **turn L** and continue for ¼ mile to the bridge that crosses the River Ribble, where **turn R** onto the B6479 (signposted Langcliffe/Stainforth/Horton in Ribblesdale). Proceed for 2 miles until you reach Stainforth, where **turn R** onto a minor road (signposted Halton Gill/Arncliffe). Ride through the village and where the road bends around to the left, **fork R** (signposted Halton Gill/Arncliffe) and engage lowest gear to climb out of the village.

The route now takes to more scenic roads with a steady climb through an area known as Silverdale. As you ride along the tops, the left-hand side provides you with spectacular views across to Pen-y-ghent as the road passes very close to the peak before descending to the T-junction in Halton Gill, where **turn R** (signposted Litton/Arncliffe).

The ride now passes through Littondale for the next 4½ miles, following the River Skirfare for much of its passage. On arriving at Arncliffe, follow the road round to the right (signposted Kilnsey/Grassington) and continue to the T-junction opposite Mitton Cottage, where **turn R** (signposted Malham) and ride past the village green. *The Falcon pub on your left-hand side serves food if you require refreshments before tackling the toughest section of the ride.*

Continue past the green, go over the bridge, follow the road round to the left and engage lowest gear to climb the 1:6 hill out of the village. Continue for 2 miles with a tricky descent to Darnbrook. At the bottom of the hill, you will

Halton Gill

have to dismount and open the gate that blocks the road in order to go on. Please remember to shut the gate behind you! Continue for a further 2½ miles to where the road divides. *For Malham Tarn Field Centre,* **turn L** *(signposted); the road takes you directly to the Centre. To rejoin the main ride, just retrace your route.*

Follow the road round to the right (signposted Settle/Malham) and in ½ mile where the road divides, **fork R** (signposted Settle) and in another ½ mile,

fork R again (signposted Langcliffe/Settle). Continue for just over 1 mile and where the road divides again, this time **fork L** (signposted Langcliffe/Settle) and continue for 3 miles to the T-junction with the B6479 in Langcliffe. Be very careful on the 1:4 (25%) hair-pin bend descent into Langcliffe. *While passing through the village, look out for the last house on the right before the T-junction (opposite Cock House) and the Naked Lady plaque on the wall dated 1660.*

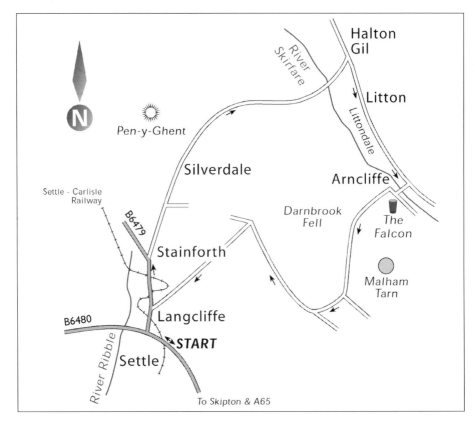

The Falcon pub at Arncliffe

Turn L onto the B6479 (signposted Settle) and descend to a T-junction in Settle. **Turn L** (signposted Skipton A65/Town Centre) to return to the car park.

• •

HALTON GILL
Halton Gill is one of the most isolated villages in Yorkshire and its loneliness is apparent on the descent from the Stainforth road. Situated at the head of Littondale, the picturesque little village nestles below the 1,800 ft peak of Horse Head Moor. Most of the houses and farms here date back to the 17th century and in the winter piles of wood and logs stand outside some of the buildings. In the olden days, the village's small population

was granted permission to coppice the trees and gather firewood, while those who lived close to the moors had the right of turbary (digging peat for fuel).

ARNCLIFFE
Arncliffe derives its name from Saxon times when the valley of Littondale was known as Amerdale. The church of St Oswald is dated to the 12th century and contains a list of the men who fought at the battle of Flodden Field in 1513. When the author Charles Kingsley came to stay with the Hammond family at Bridge End House, he was so taken with this small settlement that it became the location of his book *The Water Babies* (1863).

You can't miss the entrance to the Watershed Mill Craft Centre at Settle!

16
Settle

12, 19 or 25 miles

Based almost entirely on country lanes with no major climbs, this ride is through rolling pasture and farmland to visit the pretty little villages around the Settle area. Leaving Settle over the River Ribble and through ancient Giggleswick, the route includes Austwick with its attractive village greens, the packhorse bridge and waterfall at Stainforth, and Rathmell, where there is a horses' health farm! The three different lengths make this a suitable alternative for those unable to tackle the more difficult rides described in Routes 15 and 17, while enjoying many of the same sights.

Maps: OS Landranger 98 Wensleydale and Upper Wharfedale and 103 Blackburn and Burnley (GR 818639).

Starting point: Settle coach park, which is also a 24-hour car park (pay-and-display).

Refreshments: There are several cafés and inns in Settle, while en route pubs at Austwick and Wigglesworth both serve food and Rathmell has a tearoom.

The route: The road rises slowly after leaving Giggleswick, but whichever of the three versions you choose to ride it will be by far the easiest of the routes from Settle.

On leaving the car park, **turn L** and continue for over ¼ mile to Giggleswick. When you reach Settle Area Swimming Pool, **turn R** (signposted Stackhouse/Little Stainforth) and continue for nearly 3½ miles to a T-junction. **Turn L** onto another minor road, following the signposts for Cycle Route 68, and proceed for 2½ miles to Austwick. Continue through the village and on arriving at the T-junction beside the village green memorial, **turn L** onto a minor road (signposted Settle) and proceed for about ¾ mile to crossroads with the A65. Go straight on onto a minor road (no signpost) and continue for 2½ miles to another crossroads. Go straight on (signposted Settle) and continue for 1¼ miles.

12 mile route: Continue on the same road for a further ½ mile to crossroads with the A65. Go straight on (no signpost) and continue to a mini-roundabout. Continue straight on (signposted Settle) for ¾ mile, ignoring all turns, to a T-junction opposite the police station in Settle. **Turn L** to return to the car park.

While riding past Settle's Market Square, you pass the Naked Man Café with its plaque, on the left-hand side.

19 and 25 mile routes: **Turn R** (this turn is on a left-hand bend and easily missed, particularly as it is not signposted!) onto another minor road and continue for 4½ miles to a T-junction. After 2 miles on this stretch, you have to pass through a couple of gates in order

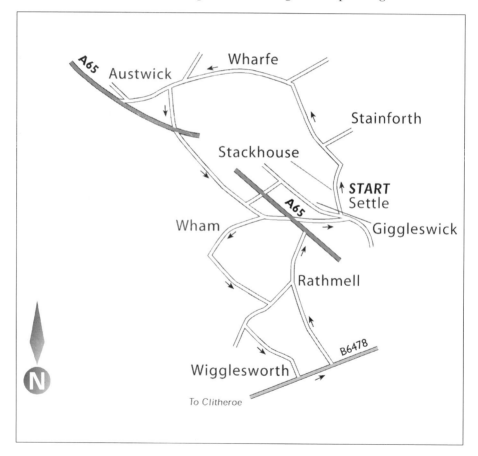

The Old School at Giggleswick

to proceed further so you will have to dismount – please remember to shut both gates behind you.

25 mile route: **Turn R** at the T-junction and continue for 1 mile, where **turn L** and proceed for 1 mile. **Turn L** and proceed for 2 miles to a T-junction with the B6478 in Wigglesworth. On this section, you will have to pass through some more gates! **Turn L** (no signpost) onto the B6478 and in about ¼ mile where the road divides beside the Plough Inn, **turn L** (signposted Rathmell/Settle) and proceed for 2 miles to Rathmell. For details of how to return to Settle, continue from ** below.

19 mile route: **Turn L** at the T-junction (signposted Rathmell/Giggleswick/ Wigglesworth) and continue to a T-junction in Rathmell. **Turn L** (no signpost). Continue at **.

Both routes: ** Drop down the hill out of the village and continue for 1¾ miles to a

A welcoming café in Settle

T-junction with the A65. **Turn L** onto the A65, followed by an immediate **turn R** onto a minor road (signposted Giggleswick/Settle) and continue for nearly ¾ mile to a mini-roundabout in Giggleswick. **Turn R** (signposted Settle) and continue for ¾ mile, ignoring all turns, to a T-junction in Settle. **Turn L** to return to the car park.

• •

SETTLE

Settle is one of Yorkshire's most popular tourist attractions. Originally a Saxon settlement, the market town contains two churches, a museum and a craft centre, but two of the most interesting places are the Folly, built in 1675 and so-named because its builder Thomas Preston lacked the money to finish it, although it has since been restored, and the impressive two-storey Shambles, which is situated in the main square. Also in the square is the Elizabethan town hall and opposite stands Ye Olde Naked Man Café, formerly an inn. The effigy above the door is dated to 1663 and it is said that the owner gave the building its name as a protest against the ornate fashions of the time. He is known as the Naked Man but on the plaque, which is in the shape of a coffin, he is depicted wearing britches and a buttoned tunic! Settle received its market charter in 1249; market day is Tuesday and the stalls are situated in the main square in front of the Shambles. The Museum of North Craven Life displays aspects of life in the Yorkshire Dales over the centuries. One of the most notable features just outside the town is the giant Castleberg Crag, which towers overhead and offers spectacular views across to the Lancashire hills of Pendle and Bowland.

GIGGLESWICK

Only separated from Settle by the River Ribble, Giggleswick has 17th century cottages, a 15th century church, a tithe barn and the well known public school. The church is dedicated to St Alkelda, who was said to have been an Anglo-Saxon princess and martyr, strangled for her faith. A Victorian dome, built to commemorate the diamond jubilee of Queen Victoria, dominates the school, founded by James Carr in 1512.

STAINFORTH

Stainforth's packhorse bridge was built around 1670 and Stainforth Force, an impressive waterfall, can be found 300 yards downstream. Most of the buildings in the village are of 19th century construction as much of the old settlement was destroyed during the Civil War.

AUSTWICK

Austwick is fortunate enough to have two greens, and you can also admire the church, or perhaps visit Austwick Hall or the local pub – the Game Cock Inn. On the wall in the pub is a poster commemorating the total eclipse of the sun that passed over the area on 29 June 1927.

RATHMELL

This small village contains many 17th century buildings and the oldest farm dates back to 1689. Rathmell also contains the Horses' Health Farm, which was established in 1991 with the sole purpose of providing treatment for horses and ponies, and visitors can watch the horses using their swimming pool.

17
The Malham Tarn Circuit
15 or 16 miles

This ride sets off north from Settle through the pretty little village of Langcliffe before climbing up onto the top of Malham Moor. To give you the chance to see the great white cliff of Malham Cove and Malham Tarn, it offers an alternative route before passing through the twin villages of Malham and Kirkby Malham and returning to Settle on a back road.

Map: OS Landranger 98 Wensleydale and Upper Wharfedale (GR 818639).

Starting point: Settle coach park, which is also a pay-and-display car park.

Refreshments: As well as pubs and cafés in Settle, there are pubs in Langcliffe and Kirkby Malham which serve food, and at least two cafés and a pub in Malham.

The route: Although not as physically demanding as Route 15, there are still some testing climbs, particularly after the villages of Langcliffe and Kirkby Malham. Be extra careful if it is windy as the tops around Malham Moor can be very exposed!

On leaving the car park, **turn L** and continue for ¼ mile until you reach the bridge over the River Ribble, where **turn R** onto the B6479 (signposted Langcliffe/Stainforth/Horton in Ribbesdale). Continue for nearly ¾ mile, passing Watershed Mill Craft Centre before a short climb to Langcliffe. On reaching the junction at the top of the hill, **turn R** onto a minor road (signposted Malham/Langcliffe). *As you ride through Langcliffe, if you look at the first house on the left (opposite Cock House), you'll see the Naked Lady plaque on the wall! This is thought to have been a sign indicating an undertaker's or carpenter's business.*

Continue through Langcliffe and, on leaving the village, engage lowest gear to climb the steep 1:5

Malham Cove

(20%) hill. As you climb the hill, Ingleborough can be seen off to your left as its distinctive shape emerges over the horizon. Continue for 3 miles to a T-junction. The ride becomes much easier now on this scenic road across the tops of Malham Moor, where Yorkshire's limestone crags become increasingly evident and Malham Tarn comes onto the horizon. At the T-junction, **turn R** (no signpost) and continue for just over 1 mile. Where the road divides, **fork R** (no signpost) and continue for another ½ mile to crossroads.

***15 mile route:* Turn R** (signposted Malham) and continue to Malham village. As you descend the steep hill into the village, Malham Cove gradually becomes visible off to your left-hand side – it is easily accessible from this route. Continue below **.

16 mile route: At the crossroads, go straight on (no signpost) and continue for 1½ miles. After about 1 mile, the road is gated so you might have to dismount in order to pass through and if so, please remember to close the gate behind you. After a further ½ mile, follow the road round to the right (signposted Malham). Continue now for 2 miles (the last mile is all downhill) and, eventually, you'll come to a T-junction where you **turn R** (signposted to the village centre) and continue to another T-junction opposite the Buck Inn, where you **turn L** (signposted to Skipton/Settle) and it's here where you will rejoin route A.

Both routes: ** Leave the village by continuing straight ahead and proceed for 1¼ miles to Kirkby Malham. Where the road bends round to the left, **fork R** (signposted Settle) and engage lowest gear to climb the 1:6 hill out of the village. Continue for 2 miles to a T-junction, where **turn R** (signposted Settle) and continue to a T-junction in Settle. You will pass the Folly off to your right as you descend the cobbled streets. **Turn R** to return to the car park.

MALHAM

Malham attracts half a million visitors a year because of the

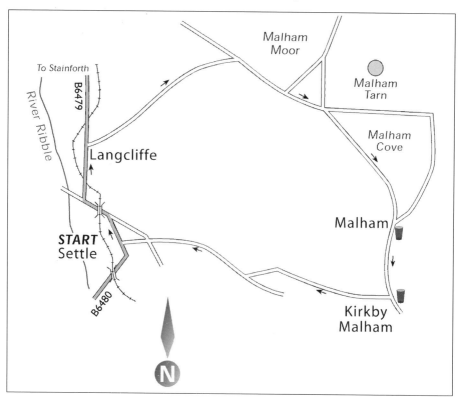

Malham Tarn

natural features that surround it. The most distinctive is Malham Cove, an 80 ft high, 900 ft wide cliff formed after the last Ice Age. Three miles to the north lies Malham Tarn, a glacial lake which, by way of an underground stream, is the source of the River Aire. The pub in the village, the Lister Arms, dates back to at least 1723.

KIRKBY MALHAM

The huge church was built to serve the widely scattered parish and the name of the village comes from Danish roots, meaning 'church place in Malhamdale'. Some of the stone cottages date from the 17th century.

(18)

Ingleton

15 miles

This route gives cyclists the opportunity to ride some of the lanes through the rolling pastureland on the western fringe of the Yorkshire Dales National Park. It visits High Bentham and the isolated settlement of Keasden at the foot of Burn Moor, before returning through Clapham to Ingleton, nestled beneath a 2,000 ft high peak. This is a lovely area with many caves and waterfalls.

Map: OS Landranger 98 Wensleydale and Upper Wharfedale (GR 695731).

Starting point: Ingleton pay-and-display car park in the village centre.

Refreshments: Ingleton has a café and pubs serving food, and at High Bentham and Clapham there are cafés that welcome cyclists.

The route: The terrain is varied but not difficult; this is one of the easier rides in the book.

Leave the car park at the eastern exit and at the T-junction, **turn R** (signposted Village Centre/Kendal/Skipton) and continue to the crossroads. Go straight on (signposted Kendal A65). Continue to the next crossroads with the A65, beside the Masons Arms, where continue straight on onto a minor road (Tatterthorn Lane). The ride now follows this minor road for the next 2½ miles, ignoring all turns.

When you reach a T-junction with the B6480, **turn R** (signposted Bentham/ Wennington/Lancaster). Continue to High Bentham. At the junction beside the Black Bull, **turn L** (signposted Station/Business Park/Slaidburn). Follow this road for about 1 mile, beginning with a descent, which is shortly

St Michael's church in the isolated village of Keasden

followed by an ascent out of the village.

On reaching the crossroads just before the Forest of Bowland sign (beside the car showroom), **turn L** (signposted Settle). Follow this country lane for the next 4 miles. It is an undulating road and gets very narrow in places so be extremely careful. This road is also gated so you may have to dismount – and please remember to close the gate behind you! You will eventually enter Keasden and pass a telephone kiosk and St Michael's church in quick succession. Shortly afterwards, **turn L** at the crossroads (signposted Clapham). Proceed for about 2 miles ignoring all turns including the left turn for Ingleton just after the railway bridge as this route uses the busy A65.

You will eventually reach a crossroads with the A65, where continue straight ahead (signposted Clapham). Continue on into Clapham to another crossroads beside the village store and packhorse bridge, where **turn L**, and shortly after passing the village store, **turn R** into Cross How Lane (signposted Bethel Chapel/Village Hall). Follow the road round to the left and engage lowest gear to climb the hill out of the village.

The ride now follows this undulating minor road back to Ingleton. It's about 4 miles, ending at a T-junction with the B6255, where **turn L** onto High Street (signposted Ingleton). Descend for a while, follow the road round to the left (signposted Village Centre), and continue past the first car park but shortly after,

just before the Ingleton Parish Regeneration Association building, **turn R** into the main car park.

INGLETON

The 2,373 ft peak of Ingleborough towers above the village of Ingleton, which has several places of interest nearby. Of the surrounding caves, the most popular are the White Scar Caves about 2 miles north-east of the village on the B6255 Ingleton–Hawes road. The caves were discovered by Christopher Long in

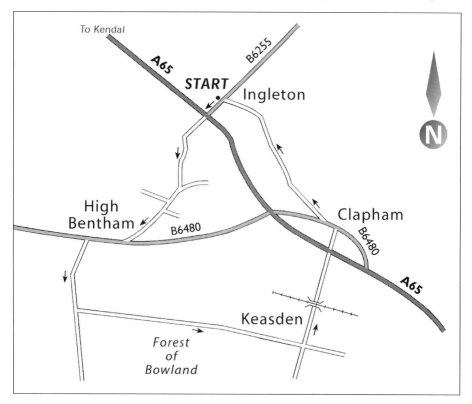

A familiar sight in the Yorkshire Dales

1923 and contain over 400 yards of footpaths. To the north are a number of waterfalls, all linked by a classic walk known as the Waterfalls Walk. The falls were discovered in the 19th century, and the walk, which is about 4 miles in length, was opened to the public in 1885. Ingleton Viaduct, built in 1860, has eleven arches and the railway was the first to carry excursion trains; the line was closed to the public in 1954.

19
Three Peaks Country
23 miles

Starting from Ingleton, this ride circles Ingleborough, arguably the most distinctive of the Three Peaks, visiting picturesque little villages as well as the Ribblehead Viaduct. After passing through the village of Helwith Bridge, the ride follows the Settle-Carlisle Railway for much of the route, passing through Ribblesdale with magnificent views extending across the Yorkshire Dales to the other two peaks of the trio, Pen-y-ghent and Whernside.

Map: OS Landranger 98 Wensleydale and Upper Wharfedale (GR 695731).

Starting point: The pay-and-display car park in the centre of Ingleton.

Refreshments: There are several cafés and pubs in Ingleton, and a pub, café, or both in every village along the route, as well as a camper van at Ribblehead that serves snacks.

The route: Although there are many climbs, this ride is not too strenuous. However, with plenty of sightseeing opportunities, it is long enough to make a challenging day's ride. Low gears will be an asset after Horton in Ribblesdale.

On leaving the car park, you will arrive at a T-junction by the viaduct, where **turn R** (signposted Cycle Route 68). Ride under the railway bridge and continue through the village. At the T-junction with the B6255, **turn L** (signposted Cycle Route 68). In ¼ mile **turn R** onto a minor road (signposted Clapham).

Continue on this country lane to the village of Clapham and where the road divides, **fork L** into Eggshell Lane (signposted Cycle Routes 10 and 68). Continue for 100 yards to the crossroads. Go straight on and follow the road round to the right into Riverside by the church. *Here, you can take a few minutes' rest to admire the waterfall on the left.* **Turn L** into

The magnificent Ribblehead Viaduct

Church Lane (signposted Austwick/Settle) and ride through the village to the T-junction by the New Inn.

Turn L onto the B6480 (no signpost, but after 100 yards a sign names it as Old Road), and continue for 1 mile to a T-junction with the A65. **Turn L** onto the A65 (signposted Settle) and in ¼ mile, **turn L** onto a minor road (signposted Austwick). Continue until you reach the traffic island opposite the telephone box in Austwick. **Turn L** onto a minor road (signposted Horton) and proceed for 3½ miles to a T-junction with the B6479 at Helwith Bridge, crossing the River Ribble just beforehand. **Turn L** onto the B6479 (signposted Horton in Ribblesdale/Hawes) and continue for 2 miles to the village of Horton in Ribblesdale. *Take note* *of how Pen-y-ghent changes shape during the journey.*

Continue through the village on the B6479, passing the Pen-y-ghent Café with its information desk. On reaching the T-junction opposite the Crown pub, **turn L** (signposted Hawes), ride over the bridge and continue for ¼ mile. At the railway station, follow the road round to the right and in ¼ mile, after passing under the railway bridge beside Blind Beck tearoom, engage lowest gear to climb the hill out of the village.

The route now follows the B6479 for 4½ miles with a series of undulations, passing through Selside at around the halfway point (the village is so tiny that if it wasn't for its extraordinary postal box and village sign you probably wouldn't notice it!). *The T-junction with the B6255 opposite the Ribblehead Viaduct is an excellent opportunity for a photograph of the viaduct with Whernside in the background.* **Turn L** onto the B6255 (signposted Ingleton) and climb the hill to the Station Inn. Low gears will be an asset on this hill.

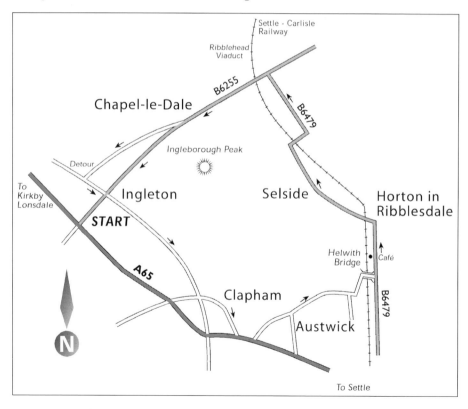

Ingleborough seen from the B6255 road

You can ride directly back to Ingleton on the B6255 if you wish, but I recommend a detour: After 2½ miles, **turn R** at the bottom of a steep hill onto a minor road (signposted Chapel-le-Dale Church) and continue for 4 miles to a T-junction in Ingleton. There are magnificent views extending towards Ingleborough as you ride alongside the River Doe. You should also be very careful on the descent into Ingleton as the road is extremely steep. **Turn L** at the T-junction to return to the village centre.

CLAPHAM
Clapham is a picturesque little village lying at the foot of Ingleborough. The Yorkshire Dales' own magazine, the *Dalesman*, was published here when it was first established in 1939. Also nearby is Ingleborough Hall, which is open to the public and has a famous garden containing many of the new species of plants introduced by Reginald Farrer, the botanist, who was born in the village and lived here. Another claim to fame is that Michael Farraday, the pioneer of modern electricity, was the son of the village blacksmith.

The church of St Oswald at Horton in Ribblesdale

HORTON IN RIBBLESDALE

Horton in Ribblesdale is the most popular starting point for walkers on the classic Three Peaks Walk. The 2,273 ft peak of Pen-y-ghent towers above the village, which is also popular with potholers. The most famous potholes are Long Churn and Alum Pot, which is 300 ft deep and said to be large enough to hold St Paul's Cathedral. The church of St Oswald dates back to the 12th century and is easily recognised off to your right as you enter the village. Its roof is made from Dales lead and there are some splendid examples of stained-glass.

20

Dent and Kingsdale

29 miles

A circuit of the western Dales that starts on the Cumbria/ Lancashire border, with a flattish ride through Lancashire before entering the Yorkshire Dales National Park near Ingleton. It's then hilly country lanes virtually all the way back to Kirkby Lonsdale, passing through Kingsdale, Dentdale and Barbondale, with wonderful views to enjoy.

Maps: OS Landranger 97 Kendal and Morecambe and 98 Wensleydale and Upper Wharfedale (GR 613784).

Starting point: The main square in Kirkby Lonsdale, which is also a car park.

Refreshments: Kirkby Lonsdale has several cafés and pubs around the main square. En route, there are cafés in Barbon, Dent, Ingleton, Burton in Lonsdale, Tunstall and Nether Burrow.

The route: Rolling most of the way through Cumbria and Yorkshire and low gears will be an asset on the climbs out of Thornton in Lonsdale and Dent, although the first few miles through Lancashire, on main roads, are relatively flat.

Turn L out of the car park and on reaching the T-junction with the A65, **turn L** (signposted Skipton). Proceed on the A65 for about ½ mile and at the junction with the A683, **turn R** (signposted Lancaster). The ride now follows the A683 for the next few miles as far as Cantsfield. Where the road divides, **fork L** onto the A687 (signposted Skipton/Settle).

Follow the A687 for about 5 miles, passing through Burton in Lonsdale and eventually returning to meet the A65. Continue straight on at the junction onto a minor road (signposted Thornton in Lonsdale) and take the **first L** (signposted Dent/Thornton in Lonsdale). At the junction beside the Marton Arms Hotel, **turn R** (signposted Dent). Engage lowest gear to climb the hill. It is about 1 mile to the top but after the initial climb the road becomes more rolling as the ride passes through an area known as Kingsdale. The road is gated in parts so you will have to dismount a couple of times, and please remember to close the gates behind you.

After a few miles, you will be rewarded for all your hard work as the road plummets down into Dentdale, but be very careful on the descent, particularly if the road surface is wet, as it is very steep in places with gradients at 1:4 (25%) on the hairpin bends. Towards the end of the descent, **turn L** at the T-junction (signposted Gawthrop/Sedbergh) and continue to Dent village about 1 mile away. *There are tearooms here if you need refreshment after a tough section, but be careful riding over the cobbles, particularly if it is wet.*

At the T-junction opposite the

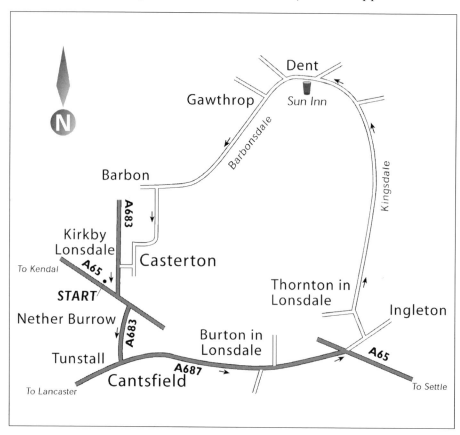

Adam Sedgwick Memorial Fountain, **turn L**. Proceed for about 1 mile and then **turn L** (signposted Gawthrop/Barbon) and engage lowest gear to climb the steep hill. In about ½ mile, **turn L** (signposted Barbon/Kirkby Lonsdale). After reaching the top of this hill, the ride passes through Barbondale. This is a very scenic valley and it is a 5-mile stretch to the next junction.

Turn L (signposted Casterton/Kirkby Lonsdale) and on reaching the T-junction, **turn R** (signposted Kirkby Lonsdale). At the next T-junction, **turn L**. This is the A683, although there is no signpost at the junction to denote this. Continue to a T-junction with the A65, where **turn R** and retrace your initial route, following the signposts back into Kirkby Lonsdale.

The Adam Sedgwick memorial in Dent

KIRKBY LONSDALE

This small town on the Yorkshire/Cumbria/Lancashire border has held a market every Thursday for over 700 years. The main street is a picturesque jumble of houses several hundred years old. Kirkby Lonsdale has won the Britain in Bloom competition three times, and twice annually the town holds a Victorian Fair, usually on the first weekend in September and

again in December for the Yuletide Procession through the streets.

DENT

Dent is often described as the Yorkshire Dales' bonniest village. It is certainly a chocolate box setting, home to the highest railway station in Britain (although it is situated 5 miles to the east of the village). Adam Sedgwick, the pioneer of modern geology, was born here in 1785 and on the main street stands a memorial fountain of pink granite.